T0244777

The National Trust

GARDENER'S
ALMANAC
2025

The National Trust

GARDENER'S
ALMANAC
2025

Greg Loades

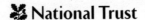
National Trust

Published by National Trust Books
An imprint of HarperCollins Publishers
1 London Bridge Street, London SE1 9GF
www.harpercollins.co.uk

HarperCollins Publishers
Macken House
39/40 Mayor Street Upper
Dublin 1, D01 C9W8, Ireland

First published in 2024
© National Trust Books 2024
Text © Greg Loades
Illustrations © Joanna Lisowiec

Weather data supplied by the Met Office © Crown copyright 2024, the Met Office

ISBN 978-0-00-864134-4
10 9 8 7 6 5 4 3 2 1

Printed in the UK using 100% Renewable Electricity at CPI Group (UK) Ltd

If you would like to comment on any aspect of this book, please contact us at the
above address or national.trust@harpercollins.co.uk

National Trust publications are available at National Trust shops or online at
Nationaltrustbooks.co.uk

Please check ahead before attending annual events and happenings listed in this book.

This book contains FSC™ certified paper and other controlled
sources to ensure responsible forest management.

For more information visit: www.harpercollins.co.uk/green

❧ CONTENTS ❧

❧ INTRODUCTION ❧

At the start of every year I tell myself that in this one I shall be more efficient. I'll sow the right things at the right time, rearrange the layout of the garden to make it more pleasing on the eye, promptly plant displays of bulbs and cut flowers, and so on. It's easy to conjure a plan when hunkered down in midwinter, with time for dreaming and reflection perhaps in more plentiful supply than usual. But later in the year the reality is quite different.

This is because the thing I don't have up my sleeve when planning in winter is that burst of energy that seems indiscriminately to be injected into every living thing in spring, whether it's seed, weed, tree or gardener: that wonderful feeling of the lights being turned on, of new life springing forth yet again. As a new growing season begins, January's to-do list is often lost amid the excitement of spring.

But it doesn't matter. As the year progresses, many things will be done in the garden that didn't come to mind in winter. New plants will be discovered, new seeds swapped, and new inspiration found from a random garden visit.

Still, the more reminders we have of what to do when in the garden, the more tangible rewards we are likely to enjoy, whether in the form of beautiful flowers or satisfying home-grown food. In the past I've sunk my fork into the ground on Christmas Day in the hope of a good parsnip harvest, wondering why I didn't sow more in April. No doubt I used the excuse that life got 'too busy'. And sometimes it does. But hopefully, with this almanac in hand, we'll still find the time.

Regardless of what sort of gardeners we are – whether tidy, fussy, messy, careful, risk-taking, traditional, trendy, lazy or industrious – and what we get done, let's enjoy the simple wonder of growing things and having the privilege of a space, whatever size it is, to nurture living things.

Happy gardening.

Greg Loades

Handkerchief tree
(*Davidia involucrata*),
see page 86.

Savoy cabbages

January

'I love flowers that bloom in winter.
Each one is a thrill, and I think we get
as much pleasure from one tiny bloom
on a winter's day as we do from a
gardenful of roses in summer.'
– Margery Fish

New Year's resolutions have never worked for me, but the year's dawn does serve as a good point for thinking about how to make a new start in the garden. There is still plenty of time before weeds begin their spring march. The garden is at its barest, giving the gardener time to pause and reflect on how and what to do to improve the space. You may even get a dry spell where things like marking out new paths or seating areas are possible. Although be prepared for snow to cover your tracks! Spending even a few minutes in the garden to dream of the year to come has a special poignancy while the garden is dormant. With few signs of life, there is a peace and tranquillity to the place that can be lacking during the growing season.

Location	Date	Rise	Set
Belfast			
	Jan 01 (Wed)	08:46 GMT	16:08 GMT
	Jan 11 (Sat)	08:40 GMT	16:23 GMT
	Jan 21 (Tue)	08:29 GMT	16:40 GMT
	Jan 31 (Fri)	08:14 GMT	17:00 GMT
Cardiff			
	Jan 01 (Wed)	08:18 GMT	16:14 GMT
	Jan 11 (Sat)	08:14 GMT	16:27 GMT
	Jan 21 (Tue)	08:05 GMT	16:43 GMT
	Jan 31 (Fri)	07:52 GMT	17:00 GMT
Edinburgh			
	Jan 01 (Wed)	08:43 GMT	15:49 GMT
	Jan 11 (Sat)	08:37 GMT	16:04 GMT
	Jan 21 (Tue)	08:25 GMT	16:23 GMT
	Jan 31 (Fri)	08:08 GMT	16:44 GMT
London			
	Jan 01 (Wed)	08:06 GMT	16:02 GMT
	Jan 11 (Sat)	08:02 GMT	16:15 GMT
	Jan 21 (Tue)	07:53 GMT	16:30 GMT
	Jan 31 (Fri)	07:39 GMT	16:48 GMT

❧ WEATHER CHARTS ❧

January averages 1991–2020

Location

Belfast	Max temperature (°C)	8.20
	Min temperature (°C)	2.18
	Days of air frost (days)	7.47
	Sunshine (hours)	40.12
	Rainfall (mm)	88.51
	Days of rainfall ≥1 mm (days)	14.44
Cardiff	Max temperature (°C)	8.58
	Min temperature (°C)	2.5
	Days of air frost (days)	7.8
	Sunshine (hours)	53.53
	Rainfall (mm)	126.97
	Days of rainfall ≥1 mm (days)	15.6
Edinburgh	Max temperature (°C)	7.29
	Min temperature (°C)	1.67
	Days of air frost (days)	9.03
	Sunshine (hours)	55.17
	Rainfall (mm)	64.66
	Days of rainfall ≥1 mm (days)	12.43
London	Max temperature (°C)	7.46
	Min temperature (°C)	2.29
	Days of air frost (days)	7.92
	Sunshine (hours)	60.02
	Rainfall (mm)	69.54
	Days of rainfall ≥1 mm (days)	12.07

❧ TASKS ❧

Things to start

Broad beans

I'm sure that broad beans were the first seeds I ever grew.
If memory serves me right I was at school, pushing these
chunky seeds into a plastic cup (or was it the inside of a
toilet roll?) of compost. As much as sowing this summer
vegetable is something of a rite of passage for young
budding gardeners, it is also an uplifting and satisfying task
for a cold winter's day. It's a definite 'heavyweight' crop
to get underway, rather than a 'something to do because
it's winter' exercise. Sow them into trays of multi-purpose
peat-free compost, one seed per module, placing them at a
depth equal to twice the height
of the seed. Water them in and
keep them in a well-lit porch
or a cold greenhouse. You'll
end up with some strong,
stout-looking young plants
that can be hardened off
for a week or so and then
planted into the ground in
April to get a head start on
spring-sown seeds.

> **Trivia**
> Greek philosopher
> Pythagoras had an intense
> dislike of broad beans,
> forbidding his followers
> from eating them or even
> touching the plants.

Hippeastrum

Perhaps you tore open some
wrapping paper to reveal some *Hippeastrum* (amaryllis)
bulbs on Christmas Day and were a little disappointed.
Still, once the dust settles on the festivities and the flashier
presents, you'll be glad of something to pot up, with the

13

promise of spectacular indoor flowers to lift the spirits before spring arrives.

- Plant your bulbs in a pot slightly wider than the bulb, with two-thirds of the bulb above the surface. For best results, use a soil-based potting compost, rather than the compost supplied in the pack.
- Water lightly after planting the bulb and keep it on a well-lit windowsill at around 20°C (68°F); water in small amounts until green shoots appear.
- Once growth has begun, give the compost a soak each time it dries. Insert a short cane into the compost to support the main stem if it looks a bit wobbly.
- As the flower begins to open, move the pot to a slightly cooler place so that the flower lasts as long as possible.

Things to finish

Savoy cabbages

These crinkly, dark green footballs are a thing of beauty in the garden and they look exquisite when covered in crisp hoar frost – so much so that it can seem a shame to harvest them! As long as they don't have the colour cooked out of them, freshly harvested Savoys make a winter roast dinner a bit more special, not to say healthier. Cut them off at the base with a sharp knife, and remove the outer leaves, which will be a bit tough. If you have chickens, toss these leaves into their run and watch them chase each other for this green bounty, which is useful roughage for them. Give the cabbages a rinse using, if possible, an outside tap before taking them in as they are likely to house a lot of little slugs.

> *'To my mind, no winter garden
> is complete without a row of mighty
> Savoy cabbages standing proud in the
> harshest weather.'*
> – Rekha Mistry

Jerusalem artichokes

Like parsnips, and many leeks and brassicas, Jerusalem artichokes are one of those handy crops that you can 'keep refrigerated' outside and just dig up as and when you need them. Very useful for saving space in the fridge or larder, and also a great excuse to get out in the garden on a cold winter's day when – to be honest – sometimes a reason is needed. Once you begin lifting these tubers with a fork, you'll probably start noticing lots of things that would have passed you by if you opted to stay indoors – maybe some lively worms, new shoots on roses or keen dandelions. Just dig up as many tubers as you want to cook, for maximum freshness. A few sliced and thrown into a roasting tin with cubes of swede and 'Maris Piper' potatoes is a real winter treat, adding comfort to dark days.

❧ SOMETHING TO SAVOUR ❦

The first signs of bulb foliage

Noticing new shoots of snowdrops, aconites, daffodils, or even tulips if it's mild, pushing their way through the soil in barren borders or previously lifeless pots is surely a more exciting new beginning than seeing the calendar roll over to 1 January. The physical signs of bulbs growing above the soil or compost surface says 'Happy New Year' with far more credibility than the finishing off of another slurred and off-key 'Auld Lang Syne'. They could yet be smothered in snow or literally frozen in time if a cold snap halts their march, but that first feeling that the garden is on the move is a special one, not to be forgotten.

HEAD GARDENER'S PLANT
❧ OF THE MONTH – JANUARY ❧

Galanthus 'Richard Ayres', chosen by David Jordan, Senior Gardener at Anglesey Abbey, Cambridgeshire

This snowdrop can be found in the Winter Garden at Anglesey Abbey, as well as in the Snowdrop Collection, an area only accessible on guided tours. Snowdrops flower in that period of dark days and long nights and bring hope for the spring to come. 'Richard Ayres' blooms especially early. It is a double snowdrop, with between three and five white outer tepals, and a multitude of inner tepals with green markings on each. It stands around 25cm (10in) tall at flowering and is generally in flower just after Christmas.

Snowdrops like a well-drained, moisture-retentive

Trivia
The name 'snowdrop' is thought to come from the resemblance of the flower to the type of pearl-drop earrings worn in Dutch painter Johannes Vermeer's *Girl with a Pearl Earring*, which were popular in the 16th and 17th centuries.

loamy soil in partial shade provided by deciduous trees. Too much shade prevents them from flowering well, so dappled shade is best. All snowdrops benefit from a top dressing of compost or leaf mould each autumn or late winter, as well as being split up when the clumps get congested to ensure good flowering.

IF YOU ONLY DO
❧ ONE THING... ❧

Plant a bare-root hedge

To be a gardener it helps to have a good imagination. Dropping seemingly lifeless sticks into cold, soggy earth might not feel like an exercise in adding blossom, berries and birds to your garden, but that's precisely what you are doing when you plant a bare-root hedge.

- Start by levelling the ground where you to intend to plant your hedge by raking it over and making sure that any perennial weeds are uprooted. Bear in mind how wide you wish the hedge to grow before deciding where to plant your hedging.
- Place each bare-root plant so that the 'nursery line', where the bottom of the stem shows two different colours, is at soil level. Break up the soil well at the base of the hole before planting.
- Firm in each plant well with the ball of your foot and water it in. Unless it is exceptionally dry and the soil becomes dusty, there is no need to water again until spring.

❧ PRUNING MADE SIMPLE ❧

Wisteria

A simple tidy-up now will help to ensure that each wisteria flower is shown off in all its glory this coming May, when you can admire that 'chocolate-box' look that makes this such a timeless, romantic climber. Use a pair of sharp secateurs (winter is a great time to sharpen and clean cutting tools) to trim back the shoots growing from the main stems. Cut them all back to two or three buds and the job is done! If you have stray side shoots growing into gutters, prune these out completely.

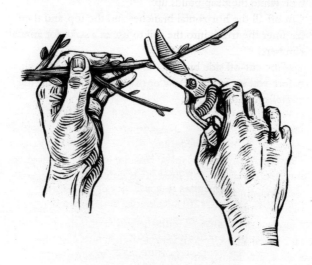

❧ RECYCLING PROJECT ❧

Ways to recycle your Christmas tree

- Saw up the trunk and stack the sawn logs into a pile in a damp, sheltered corner of the garden to encourage frogs and toads.
- Cut the branches off and put them through a shredder, then use the chopped material as a mulch for rhododendrons or blueberries.
- Cut thin branches into 15cm (6in) long lengths and use them to line the bottom of a new compost heap. They will eventually break down but will allow air to circulate at the base while the heap builds up.
- Cut off all the horizontal branches and the top, and then hammer the trunk into the soil to use as a stake for annual climbers.
- Use the cut-off side branches to cover areas of bare soil before you are ready to sow or plant, to keep cats off the empty ground.

Trivia
The world's tallest cut Christmas tree was a 64.6m (212ft) tall Douglas fir (Pseudotsuga menziesii) which stood in Northgate shopping centre, Seattle, Washington, USA, during Christmas 1950.

❧ CROP OF THE MONTH ❧

Kale

While we probably associate cut-and-come-again crops with summer, kale is one that does the trick in winter. Harvesting the main crown of the plant at the end of autumn allows smaller shoots to gradually take their place. Cut off a few young shoots when they are around 10cm (4in) long, or cut off the whole leaf rosette in one go and the plant should sprout some new growth that can be harvested before winter is out. If we hit a frosty spell, just admire the form of these statuesque plants and harvest from them when they've thawed. Vegetables are underrated for their ornamental value in winter, with kale leading the way, along with leeks and Savoy cabbages, which can easily upstage ornamental grasses and perennial seedheads for their architectural merits.

HOUSEPLANT
❧ OF THE MONTH ❧

Indoor azalea

If you don't have acid soil and haven't enough room on the patio to dedicate to these woodland shrubs, growing azaleas as houseplants is another option. The beauty of these colourful evergreens indoors is that they thrive in cool temperatures, making them perfect for those chilly bathrooms or porches that can end up being houseplant graveyards! A humid place at 13–16°C (55–61°F) should be perfect for these plants, and regular misting to maintain humidity will help to keep them happy. These plants may have been grown in a warmer environment where they were

sold or raised, in order to encourage early blooming, so
the plant may take a while to settle down and rebloom in
future years.

❧ HOW TO HELP WILDLIFE ❧

Plant some berried shrubs
While ornamental berries are most noticeable in the garden
in winter, when their bright colours stand out starkly during
the barest time of year, with some considered planting this
month we can ensure that there are berries available in the
garden for much longer. They provide valuable food for
birds, and dormice and wood mice enjoy nibbling on berries
from the garden too. When it's dry enough underfoot to not
be sliding about and making mud, it's a good time to plant
some berry-rich shrubs. If you can dig into the soil without
it sticking to your spade, then you're good to go. For some
summer berries try growing a black elder (*Sambucus nigra*
'Black Lace'); for fruits in autumn grow the gorgeous spindle
(*Euonymus europaeus*); and for winter you are spoilt for
choice. The spiny blackthorn (*Prunus spinosa*) will give you a
crop of sloes to share with the thrushes.

❧ BIRD OF THE MONTH ❧

Redwing
If we get a snowfall that leaves fields covered in a blanket
of white then this little bird, the smallest true thrush, may
venture into gardens that are still offering a glimpse of berry-
strewn greenery on hawthorns or windfallen apples amid the
winter's snow. Identify it by the creamy yellow stripe above

its eye, the orangey-yellow colouring around its wings and its high-pitched call, which is reminiscent of a referee's first blow into a whistle.

WILD IN THE GARDEN
❧ THIS MONTH ❧

Rabbits
You could see a rabbit at any time and their breeding season begins this month. There is a good chance you will notice their work – stripped tree bark – especially at this time of year, before you see the creatures themselves. Taut wire

netting barriers can keep them at bay, as can rabbit guards (biodegradable options are available), which are worth investing in to protect special trees and shrubs.

'There were days last winter when I danced for sheer joy out in my frost-bound garden.'
– Elizabeth von Arnim

ANNUAL EVENTS AND
❧ HIGHLIGHTS ❧

Houseplant Week, 6–12 January

Treat yourself to a new houseplant this month to lift the mood indoors and keep you in touch with growing things! It's amazing how just one plant on a windowsill can start off the excitement of another growing season being just around the corner.

Squirrel Appreciation Day, 21 January

You might think twice about joining in with this, especially if grey squirrels are a bit of a nuisance in your garden. But watching squirrels is great fun if you have children, especially if you do it at the local park and not your own garden! If you happen to spot a red squirrel then it's an increasingly rare sight, with around 120,000 in Britain compared to 2 million grey squirrels.

RSPB Big Garden Birdwatch, 25–27 January
It's time to spend an hour watching the birds that visit your garden and record the results for the RSPB. Your report helps the RSPB get a picture of which birds in the UK are endangered, helping them to act to save those that are in decline.

❧ GARDENER'S CHECKLIST ❧

☐ Keep deadheading pansies to encourage more winter blooms.

☐ Remove yellowing leaves from winter brassicas.

☐ Cover areas of bare soil with fleece or wool to warm them, after removing weeds and levelling the ground.

☐ Place a bucket over rhubarb crowns to force an early crop of fresh young stems.

☐ Remove perennial weeds now to get a head start before spring.

☐ Hang fat balls on your bird feeders.

YOUR NOTES FOR
❧ JANUARY ❧

To sow

To plant

In flower

Wildlife spotted

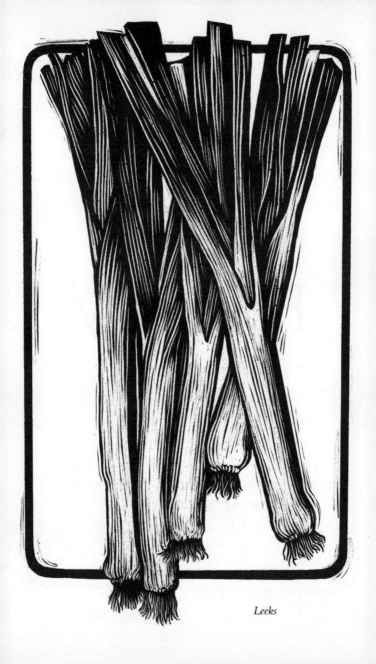

Leeks

February

'Gardens never stand still and never
allow us to buy a season ticket on the
line of least resistance.'
– Robin Lane Fox

Is there a month as difficult to read as February? Sometimes the coldest, snowiest month of the year, it can also trick us into thinking spring is close at hand, and for a fleeting few minutes you might be tempted to dispense with the jacket while pottering around on a sunny afternoon. In such an unpredictable month, one thing is certain: the daylight hours are lengthening and aconites, snowdrops, crocuses and scented deciduous shrubs will add a flurry of tiny flowers to whet the appetite for the spring moments to come. Even the coldest of Februarys can be productive indoors, with the joy of shopping for flower seeds, and starting some of them off too, especially if you've got a heated propagator to set them on their way.

❧ SUNRISE AND SUNSET 2025 ❧

Location	Date	Rise	Set
Belfast			
	Feb 01 (Sat)	08:12 GMT	17:02 GMT
	Feb 11 (Tue)	07:53 GMT	17:23 GMT
	Feb 21 (Fri)	07:31 GMT	17:44 GMT
	Feb 28 (Fri)	07:14 GMT	17:58 GMT
Cardiff			
	Feb 01 (Sat)	07:50 GMT	17:02 GMT
	Feb 11 (Tue)	07:33 GMT	17:20 GMT
	Feb 21 (Fri)	07:14 GMT	17:39 GMT
	Feb 28 (Fri)	06:59 GMT	17:51 GMT
Edinburgh			
	Feb 01 (Sat)	08:06 GMT	16:46 GMT
	Feb 11 (Tue)	07:46 GMT	17:08 GMT
	Feb 21 (Fri)	07:23 GMT	17:30 GMT
	Feb 28 (Fri)	07:06 GMT	17:45 GMT
London			
	Feb 01 (Sat)	07:38GMT	16:50 GMT
	Feb 11 (Tue)	07:21 GMT	17:08 GMT
	Feb 21 (Fri)	07:02 GMT	17:26 GMT
	Feb 28 (Fri)	06:47 GMT	17:39 GMT

❧ WEATHER CHARTS ❧

February averages 1991–2020

Location

Belfast	Max temperature (°C)	8.78
	Min temperature (°C)	2.13
	Days of air frost (days)	6.75
	Sunshine (hours)	65.16
	Rainfall (mm)	70.26
	Days of rainfall ≥1 mm (days)	12.65
Cardiff	Max temperature (°C)	9.15
	Min temperature (°C)	2.47
	Days of air frost (days)	7.27
	Sunshine (hours)	76.15
	Rainfall (mm)	92.97
	Days of rainfall ≥1 mm (days)	12.00
Edinburgh	Max temperature (°C)	7.96
	Min temperature (°C)	1.72
	Days of air frost (days)	8.84
	Sunshine (hours)	82.23
	Rainfall (mm)	53.05
	Days of rainfall ≥1 mm (days)	9.83
London	Max temperature (°C)	8.07
	Min temperature (°C)	2.25
	Days of air frost (days)	7.48
	Sunshine (hours)	76.06
	Rainfall (mm)	51.41
	Days of rainfall ≥1 mm (days)	10.65

❧ TASKS ❧

Things to start

F

Asiatic lilies in pots

This is one of those 'I'm so glad I took ten minutes to do it' tasks. It is so ridiculously easy and will bring endless joy come summer. Just place three bulbs in a 30cm (12in) pot (with drainage holes in the bottom) half-filled with an equal parts mix of peat-free multipurpose compost and soil-based compost, with a handful of grit mixed in. Make sure the bulbs aren't touching, then cover with a 12cm (4¾in) layer of the compost mix and water them in. Keep in a sunny spot, ready to enjoy the exotic blooms from June to August.

Trivia
The famous Spencer sweet peas, renowned for their long stems and large blooms, were originally developed by Silas Cole, Head Gardener at Althorp Park, the country seat of Earl Spencer and the family home of Diana, Princess of Wales.

Sweet peas

There are so many windows of opportunity to sow these classic summer flowers. Any time from October to March will give you sweet-smelling bunches of blooms to fill a room with fragrance. Soak the seeds for 24 hours before sowing and push two seeds into recycled inner tubes from kitchen roll (at least 12cm/4¾in long) filled with seed-sowing compost. Cover with a compost layer equal to the height of two seeds and gently water them in. Keep them in a well-lit place indoors. Good light is more important than heat, because the seeds can germinate at low temperatures, but lack of light will lead to spindly seedlings.

Things to finish

Leeks
I always think of leeks as the 'first ones in and the last ones out'. They always seem to be in the veg patch or on the windowsill in some capacity or another. The last stems standing are best harvested now and you may need to unravel quite a few outer layers to find a firm shaft that is good for eating. Pull or dig up all that you have left and you'll have a crumbly layer of top soil left behind. The fibrous root systems of leeks leave their mark after harvesting, with a good friable soil for sowing into next month. Grow brassicas or legumes (peas and beans) in the patch this year.

'And thus the snowdrop, like the bow
That spans the cloudy sky,
Becomes a symbol whence we know,
That brighter days are nigh.'
– From 'Snowdrop' by George Wilson

Cutting back deciduous grasses
It may seem to leave a big hole in the garden all of a sudden, but there comes a point when leaving last year's foliage intact in the hope of pretty frosty pictures has to be forgotten, with the mind turning instead towards the arrival of spring and new beginnings. Taller deciduous grasses such as *Phalaris* 'Feesey' have probably collapsed into a heap by now, and as February enters its last days, cut all the old stems to ground

level. If the weather has been mild, you may well see some signs of new growth just above the soil surface. There will be a few ensuing weeks when the garden can seem a bit flat, if you've cut down a lot of old grasses, and perennials too. But you've fired a starting gun that says spring is on its way, and it's time to move on from the past. This alone makes it an exciting thing to do.

❧ SOMETHING TO SAVOUR ❧

Winter-flowering jasmine

You don't have to wait for daffodils to start blooming to get a fix of sunny yellow flowers early in the year. The bare stems of winter jasmine (*Jasminum nudiflorum*) are smothered in masses of star-shaped flowers and an established plant in full flower is a spectacular sight that will brighten a wall or fence all winter. The gangly stems do need supporting with wire or trellis but – for the most natural look – plant in an elevated place so that the shrub can tumble over a wall to show off its flowers to very good effect, like a waterfall of winter colour. Grow in sun or part shade in soil that isn't too heavy.

HEAD GARDENER'S PLANT
❧ OF THE MONTH – FEBUARY ❧

Rhododendron 'Praecox' chosen by Ned Lomax, Head Gardener at Bodnant Garden, Conwy

Planted widely around the garden, this is a perennial favourite at Bodnant. The best displays can be found in the

Winter Garden and beside the statue of Priapus at the top of the west terraces.

Clusters of lilac/purple flowers smother the plant when in full bloom, contrasting with the dark, glossy green foliage. The colour stands out particularly well in the half-light of late afternoon and works well with the yellow of early spring daffodils. Flowering so impressively for a good three-week period, 'Praecox' provides excellent value in the spring garden.

While fully hardy across most of Britain, some protection against frost will provide the best display of flowers. 'Praecox' is easily grown in moist, well-drained, slightly acidic soils. Intense summer sun should be avoided but a bright site is perfectly suitable, particularly in cooler climates.

Compact in habit and growing to around 1.5m (5ft) tall, 'Praecox' can be used to form an excellent low hedge. Although pruning isn't necessary, it responds well to being cut back to maintain a dense habit. It also benefits from a mulch and feed in the spring. Deadheading will also promote strong growth and flowering.

IF YOU ONLY DO
❧ ONE THING... ❧

Cut back buddleja

As the month slowly shuffles to its last few days, it's a good time to tackle one of the most brutal gardening tasks of the year. If left unpruned, buddlejas can begin to resemble those ungainly triffids that are unmissable by the side of railway tracks but which we perhaps like to pretend are quite different from the more refined, well-mannered versions we have in our own garden. Be ruthless and use loppers or a sharp pruning saw; cutting each stem to 10cm (4in) from ground level will result in a plant full of fresh, supple new growth that will quickly turn woody and dripping with droopy, nectar-filled flowerheads come July. This will keep your buddlejas manageable in a mixed border, where they will serve as a team player rather than a looming shade-creator. If you're looking for a new one but space is tight, try a compact form such as 'Hot Raspberry' which grows to just 90cm (3ft) tall.

Trivia
Buddlejas are named in honour of the English clergyman and botanist Adam Buddle, author of a complete English Flora, finished in 1708 but never published.

❧ PRUNING MADE SIMPLE ❦

Rose bushes

Pruning bush roses is one of those jobs that for some reason is sometimes made very complicated. This is strange because few plants are as forgiving as roses. It is not easy to kill a rose, or to lose flowers, by pruning it, so there really is little to lose and lots to gain.

- Start by cutting out all the dead stems. Check the base of the plants and cut all brown stems out right at the bottom, taking care that thorns don't scratch you (easier written than done).
- For large shrub roses, also remove up to one-third of the oldest, thickest stems at the base, then cut back the rest by about half, to leave a domed shape.
- For smaller rose bushes, cut all the stems back to 10cm (4in) from the base, making a cut just above a bud.
- If you have a shrub rose that has become a tangled thicket and has been flowering poorly, cut all the stems back to 15cm (6in) from the base.
- Once pruning is finished, clear all leaf debris and weeds from the soil around the bottom of the plant, sprinkle granular rose food over the soil and then water it in.

❧ RECYCLING PROJECT ❦

Coppice hazels

Coppicing sounds very grand, as if a job for a tree surgeon or the manager of a large estate, but all it involves is cutting back the stems of woody plants to just above ground level. With hazel, the pruned stems make sturdy supports for plants such as runner beans when tied together. Thinner growth is also usual and should be bendy enough to form arches that can be pushed into the soil to prop up border perennials.

❧ CROP OF THE MONTH ❧

Sprouting seeds and microgreens

With a few seeds and a little water, the first harvest of the year can be made this month, of succulent sprouting seeds, and you only need a tiny amount of space. Purpose-built seed-sprouters are available, but you can grow them in a recycled glass jar with a piece of muslin secured to the top with an elastic band.

HOUSEPLANT ❧ OF THE MONTH ❧

Phalaenopsis

These plants – commonly known as moth orchids – look a million dollars when you buy them in bloom. To get them to re-bloom, it's a great help if you can grow them in a room that receives natural light – in other words, somewhere where it will never be on the dark side

Trivia

Moth orchids were first identified by German-Dutch botanist Karl Ludwig Blume in the 1820s. Dr Blume likened the flowers being blown by the wind to flying white moths, so the name was born. The Greek word phalaina *means 'moth' while* opsis *means 'resembling' or 'likeness'.*

of a curtain or blind. Ideally keep the temperature above 16°C (61°F) at all times and place the plants in a room where the temperature is stable. Keep them as far away from radiators as possible, and ensure the leaves are not in direct sunlight in summer. Water once a week by pouring the water onto the roots and letting it run straight through the bottom of the pot. You won't need to water as much in winter, just check the roots and only water when they look dry rather than damp.

❧ HOW TO HELP WILDLIFE ❧

Plant early flowers in your sunny spots

Early foraging bees, such as the mining bee and red-tailed bumblebee, are looking for flowers long before much of the garden has woken from its winter sleep. Planting some early-flowering plants will give them a very welcome source of food. Winter aconites, crocuses and daffodils such as *Narcissus* 'Rijnveld's Early Sensation' can all be bought in flower, as can perennials such as pulmonaria, single-flowered hellebores and primroses. Early bees love to forage in the sun, so take a look at where the sunlight falls in your garden in early spring and make some space for early flowers there.

❧ BIRD OF THE MONTH ❧

Mistle thrush

The mistle thrush is Britain's largest songbird and gets its name for being rather partial to the berries of mistletoe. It is easily identified by its white breast, patterned with dark brown spots. This bird is something of a fighter, guarding the plants that it has decided to feed on. They will nest from now until May, building scruffy nests out of mud, moss, leaves and grass, in the forks of trees.

WILD IN THE GARDEN
❧ THIS MONTH ❧

Sweet violet (*Viola odorata*)

Very similar in appearance to the dog violet (*Viola riviniana*), the giveaway sign of finding this early-flowering beauty is the delicious scent that gives it its name. One of the first wild flowers to appear, found hugging the ground on woodland edges, it is an important food plant for early butterflies. For your own posies of these delicate blue-violet blooms at home, buy some plants from a reputable nursery rather than picking them from the wild, where they are becoming increasingly rare.

ANNUAL EVENTS AND
❧ HIGHLIGHTS ❧

Seed swaps
Early February is a good time to get the seed sowing year underway, with many summer flowers best sown soon, and tomatoes and chillies best started in the next few weeks. A seed swap event can help boost your plant stocks without having to spend a lot of money and it's a great place to meet other gardeners. Check gardenorganic.org for a seed swap event near you.

Snowdrop season
February is snowdrop season and many National Trust gardens open their gates to show off their inspiring snowdrop collections. For a bracing winter walk, adorned with beautiful flowers, head to the gardens at Kingston Lacy, Dorset, where you can follow a guided snowdrop trail, or take a stroll through Newark Park, Gloucestershire, to enjoy carpets of snowdrops and some bird spotting too.

Camellia season
The whole month is a celebration of these glorious late winter flowers at Chiswick House in west London, where their conservatory camellias, one of the oldest collections under glass in Europe, can be enjoyed.

Kew Orchid Festival, 1 February–2 March

Kew's famous festival runs throughout the month, with sensational glasshouse displays of orchids from around the world. It's a great pick-me-up on a cold winter's day and you may find it hard to resist the urge to grow them at home!

National Nestbox Week, 14–21 February

This week puts breeding birds in the spotlight and encourages everyone to put up a nest box or two in their garden. A nest box in a sheltered site is ideal, placed at least 1m (3¼ft) above ground level, and getting it in place this month will mean that it's ready well before most birds are beginning to nest.

'February is like the beginning of a party ... there is an air of hushed expectancy.'
– Ursula Buchan

❧ GARDENER'S CHECKLIST ❧

☐ Sprout or 'chit' seed potatoes in egg boxes, placing them in a well-lit, frost-free place.

☐ Lift and divide snowdrop bulbs immediately after flowering.

☐ Check winter container displays to see if they need water.

☐ Top up the grit layer around the base of alpine plants.

☐ Trim back stems that have faded on winter-flowering heathers.

☐ Weed and mulch asparagus beds while the plants are still dormant.

YOUR NOTES FOR
❧ FEBRUARY ❧

To sow

To plant

In flower

Wildlife spotted

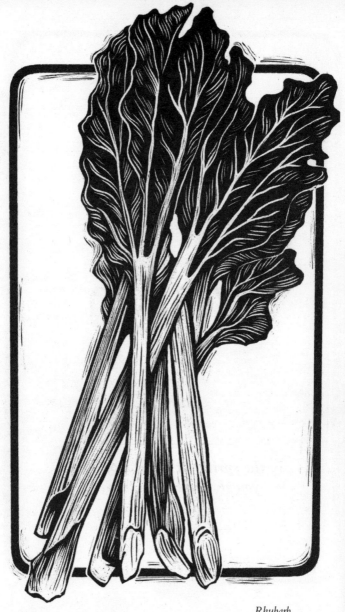

Rhubarb

March

'In the spring, at the end of the day,
you should smell like dirt.'
– Margaret Atwood

S urely a very aptly named month for gardeners, with winter's slow pace definitely replaced with a purposeful movement akin to a march: seed trays are filled, borders mulched, the ground cleared and perhaps the grass cut too. Regardless of the expected biting winds and the possibility of wintry flurries, the garden feels like it's moving forward and no longer asleep. Savour these early spring days, when great strides can be made while the weather is still cool, the ground mostly clear, and the garden refreshingly free of jobs that need urgent attention. And then there are the bulbs: when temperatures nudge up enough for daffodils to burst forth, it's like fireworks going off to welcome a new gardening year.

❧ SUNRISE AND SUNSET 2025 ❧

Location	Date	Rise	Set
Belfast			
	Mar 01 (Sat)	07:12 GMT	18:00 GMT
	Mar 11 (Tue)	06:48 GMT	18:20 GMT
	Mar 21 (Fri)	06:23 GMT	18:39 GMT
	Mar 31 (Mon)	05:57 GMT	18:58 GMT
Cardiff			
	Mar 01 (Sat)	06:57 GMT	17:53 GMT
	Mar 11 (Tue)	06:35 GMT	18:10 GMT
	Mar 21 (Fri)	06:12 GMT	18:27 GMT
	Mar 31 (Mon)	05:50 GMT	18:44 GMT
Edinburgh			
	Mar 01 (Sat)	07:03 GMT	17:47 GMT
	Mar 11 (Tue)	06:38 GMT	18:08 GMT
	Mar 21 (Fri)	06:11 GMT	18:28 GMT
	Mar 31 (Mon)	05:45 GMT	18:49 GMT
London			
	Mar 01 (Sat)	06:45 GMT	17:41 GMT
	Mar 11 (Tue)	06:23 GMT	17:58 GMT
	Mar 21 (Fri)	06:00 GMT	18:15 GMT
	Mar 31 (Mon)	05:37 GMT	18:32 GMT

❧ WEATHER CHARTS ❧

March averages 1991–2020

Location		
Belfast	Max temperature (°C)	10.48
	Min temperature (°C)	3.12
	Days of air frost (days)	4.39
	Sunshine (hours)	97.71
	Rainfall (mm)	71.37
	Days of rainfall ≥1 mm (days)	12.64
Cardiff	Max temperature (°C)	11.31
	Min temperature (°C)	3.91
	Days of air frost (days)	3.93
	Sunshine (hours)	116.59
	Rainfall (mm)	85.29
	Days of rainfall ≥1 mm (days)	12.29
Edinburgh	Max temperature (°C)	9.71
	Min temperature (°C)	2.93
	Days of air frost (days)	5.77
	Sunshine (hours)	117.32
	Rainfall (mm)	48.48
	Days of rainfall ≥1 mm (days)	9.83
London	Max temperature (°C)	10.91
	Min temperature (°C)	3.72
	Days of air frost (days)	3.69
	Sunshine (hours)	114.20
	Rainfall (mm)	42.82
	Days of rainfall ≥1 mm (days)	9.06

⚘ TASKS ⚘

Things to start

Tomatoes

The beginning of March is a good time to sow. Natural light is more plentiful and the time needed to tend young plants before frost has passed is shorter and more manageable, compared to tomatoes sown at the end of January or early February. Fill some 8cm (3in) pots with seed-sowing compost, water it, then place tomato seeds on the compost surface, leaving a gap between each seed. This will make transplanting easier later. Cover the seed with sieved compost, label the pot then keep in a propagator at 20°C (68°F) or place a clear plastic bag over the pot and secure it with an elastic band.

Gooseberries

No matter how big and how bountiful the plant, I can never have enough gooseberries. Perhaps it is because those rather portly July berries deflate like burst balloons when cooked, meaning those large bags that fill the freezer in summer give a false picture of how many desserts can be conjured up from them. But the main reason is because they have a taste like no other, and it's not really a fruit you can successfully buy from the shops – unless you have a liking for very sour, unripe fruits that are as hard as conkers. Now is a good chance to plant one. Grow in an open, sunny part

Trivia
The world's heaviest gooseberry weighed in at 64.83g (2¼oz), grown by Graeme Watson and exhibited at the Egton Bridge Gooseberry Show, North Yorkshire, UK, which has been running since 1800.

of the garden, or in a sunny place on the patio, in soil-based compost and space at least 1m (3¼ft) apart if you're growing more than one. 'Invicta' is a good choice for yield, and mature plants have good resistance to disease.

Things to finish

Cornus pruning

It's best not to leave cutting back cornus any later than mid-March because the plants will be starting to shoot. Those bare stems showing off bright colours begin to look a bit hazy as soft green shoots emerge when the weather starts to warm up, and cutting back stems full of new shoots will set the plant back and delay flowering too. To maintain a simple framework of healthy stems and the best winter colour, cut all stems back to 10cm (4in) from the base and completely remove any awkwardly placed stems, taking them down to ground level. Long pruned stems can make useful, slightly bendy supports for border perennials.

Brussels sprouts

It's time to pull up the last of the sprouts, and getting rid of these strange-looking empty stalks is a very definite statement of a new season having started. A bulky remnant of winter, clearing these plants as you snap off the final harvest not only frees up space but also makes the veg plot look instantly more spring-like, with bare soil crying out 'Start sowing soon!' Put the old stems through a shredder if you have one, or chop them up into small pieces with secateurs, or even better,

Trivia
Raw Brussels sprouts contain more Vitamin C than oranges. Eating them raw may be a step too far for some though!

a sturdy pair of loppers and add the material to the compost heap.

❧ SOMETHING TO SAVOUR ❧

The skeleton of the garden

The start of March is the last chance to see the garden in its 'asleep' state. It's an opportunity to think about whether evergreen plants or structural elements might improve the place. Maybe there's a well-trodden path that's been cheekily taken through a border or across the lawn and is compacting the ground. Could it be surfaced as a path, or more space made elsewhere to fix the issue? All these things are quickly forgotten amid the frenzy of spring and the abundant summer growth can dramatically hide the layout of the garden. The start of the month is also a good time to move shrubs, trees and roses.

M

HEAD GARDENER'S PLANT ❧ OF THE MONTH – MARCH ❧

Camellia 'Maud Messel' chosen by Joe Whelan, Head Gardener at Nymans, West Sussex

This plant was raised at Nymans and named after plant-lover Maud Messel, wife of Leonard Messel, who was Nymans' second owner. It's a prolific and reliable flowerer, with the first blooms appearing in early February but reaching their peak in March. The flowers are dark pink, and if given enough space, the plant will grow into a large, evergreen shrub around 4m (13ft) high by 3m (10ft) wide.

This camellia is found in various locations in the garden at Nymans. Our most impressive group is found marking the entrance to the Forecourt Garden adjacent to the house, a fitting location next to the garden designed by Maud Messel herself in the 1930s.

Well suited to cool, shady parts of the garden, it's happiest in acidic, well-drained soil though it will tolerate damper conditions. It benefits from a mulch to keep the roots cool. Well-rotted leaf mould works best. Camellias are generally pretty robust as long as they are planted in the right spot. They can be lightly pruned after flowering if needed; if a harder prune is required, then June is the best time so that the plant has time to recover ahead of winter.

IF YOU ONLY DO
❧ ONE THING... ❦

Sow hardy annuals
So much colour and so many flowers can come from just a few minutes of sowing hardy annuals! These flowers are tough enough to cope with the cold, so they can be sown direct outside. Wait until we reach a mild and dry spell, then sow in drifts, or in rows if you want to grow cut flowers rather than a border display. Weed the soil first, level it with a rake, and then scatter the seed and gently rake it in. Water if the soil is very dry. There's a wide range of flowers to sow this way, including nasturtiums, clarkia, pot marigold, Californian poppy, nigella, linaria and poached egg plant (*Limnanthes*).

❧ PRUNING MADE SIMPLE ❧

Hardy fuchsias

Be brave with hardy fuchsia pruning: the more brutal you are, the better the results. Take the plunge and use loppers or secateurs to cut each stem to 10cm (4in) from the base and you will be rewarded with fresh, healthy growth that will be dripping with flowers by midsummer. Cut just above a pair of leaf buds. If you are unsure whether your fuchsia has survived the winter, look out for the leaf buds beginning to emerge. If you're still not sure, scrape back the surface of a stem with your fingernail: if it's a vibrant green then the plant is still alive.

M

❧ RECYCLING PROJECT ❧

Newspaper pots

Kits for making small pots out of newspaper will help you
to raise a multitude of young plants without the need for
plastic. The pots are ideal for plants that are almost ready to
be planted out but need a bit longer in pots before going
into the soil. This way, they can be grown on and watered
a few times without the paper collapsing, and can then be
planted, pot and all, into the soil. Use them for hardy annuals
such as sunflowers or as the final pots for brassicas before
being planted out.

❧ CROP OF THE MONTH ❧

Rhubarb

As the month enters its last days, and evenings are light
enough for some serious stints of gardening, rhubarb
should be offering up some delicious-looking new growth,
especially if you covered the clump with a forcer in
January or February. It's best to have at least two clumps of
rhubarb if you have the space to spare, because they will get
exhausted by continuous harvesting. Try growing a clump
in a pot 30cm (12in) wide if you've
run out of space in the ground.
After harvesting, the large leaves
can be laid over bare soil to
perform a variety of uses,
from providing a temporary
weed-blocker, to preventing
cats from treating the space
as a WC. Pull the stems out
with a sharp tug to keep the

Trivia
*During the Second World
War the British government
classed rhubarb as an
essential food and fixed the
price of rhubarb at 1 shilling
per pound in an attempt
to keep it affordable for
everyone.*

soft and delicious, pinkish-white stem base intact. If you find rhubarb too sour, try cooking it with a stick of cinnamon, a few hearty chunks of fresh ginger and a good glug of honey.

HOUSEPLANT
❧ OF THE MONTH ❧

Tillandsia xerographica
Known as the 'king of air plants', *Tillandsia xerographica* is a real work of art. It's suitable for growing in terrariums, hanging planters or in a simple pot filled with pretty stones. In the wild it grows on high tree branches, wrapping its roots around them and taking in moisture through its foliage. With this in mind, give it a bright spot in the house, but out of direct sunlight. To water it, immerse the whole plant in a bowl of tepid rainwater for two minutes then remove it and allow it to dry before putting it back in its pot or terrarium.

'Daffodils, that come before the swallow dares,
and take the winds of March with beauty.'
– From *The Winter's Tale*, William Shakespeare

❧ HOW TO HELP WILDLIFE ❧

Plant out some more early flowers
The parts of the garden in full sun now will be significantly warmer than those in the shade and it's here that early bees

will be foraging. Take a look at the sunniest parts of the garden now and if there are gaps, it's a good time to add plants that will give March colour and flowers year after year. Visit a garden centre or nursery to see what is in flower that suits your style and soil. Pulmonaria are reliable ground-cover perennials with dainty flowers and patterned leaves, while pasqueflowers (*Pulsatilla*) add elegance in very well-drained soils, with their soft, silvery leaves. For something shrubby, flowering quince (*Chaenomeles*) will grow in more or less any soil and has white, red, pink or orangey cup-shaped flowers that look a little bit like apple blossom.

❧ BIRD OF THE MONTH ❦

Blue tit
This tiny bird will be beginning to build its nest by the end of the month and its high-pitched chirrup is a soothing balm as spring begins. Bird feeder regulars, they are partial to peanuts and fat balls. They produce one brood of chicks, raised to coincide with peak caterpillar season, so there's plenty of food to go round!

WILD IN THE GARDEN
❧ THIS MONTH ❦

Primrose
A potential indicator that you are on a site of ancient woodland, this British native wild flower is likely to be in bloom this month and can still be flowering in May.

Trivia
The leaves of the common primrose have been used to make tea, which is said to alleviate insomnia.

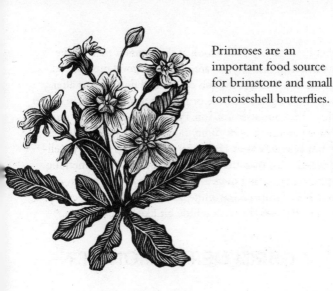

Primroses are an important food source for brimstone and small tortoiseshell butterflies.

M

ANNUAL EVENTS AND
❧ HIGHLIGHTS ❧

World Book Day, 6 March
Celebrate World Book Day by visiting one of the National Trust's second-hand bookshops. The National Trust has more than 200 shops selling quality second-hand books, including gardening books, raising money for the places in their care.

Daffodil festival, 15–23 March
Celebrate the arrival of spring at the annual Daffodil Festival at Cotehele, Cornwall, as their magnificent collection of over 300 different varieties, some dating back to the 17th century, shows off a mass of cheerful blooms.

Mothering Sunday, 30 March
Lots of the Trust's properties will be open for a family day
out and a chance to treat mum to an afternoon tea – let's
hope for some sunny weather!

Plant hunter's fairs
Look out for these fairs at a selection of venues throughout
the country, with plants from some of the best independent
nurseries in the country.

❧ GARDENER'S CHECKLIST ❧

☐ Put up plant supports for climbers and perennials
that have a habit of getting a bit top-heavy in
summer.

☐ Protect early emerging perennial shoots from slugs.

☐ Cut the old flowerheads off hydrangeas.

☐ Cover nectarine, peach and apricot blossom with
fleece if frost is forecast.

☐ Make the first lawn cut of the year, keeping blades
set high.

☐ Open greenhouse vents on mild days but shut
them before dark.

YOUR NOTES FOR
❧ MARCH ❧

To sow

To plant

In flower

Wildlife spotted

Tulips

April

'Part of the reason we garden and visit
gardens is to escape: from ugliness to
beauty, from tension to tranquillity,
from noise to peace.'
– Anna Pavord

The scents of wallflowers, mown grass, lily of the valley and warming earth are just a few of the many delights of the April garden. This is the month when things start to change visibly by the day, and anything feels possible. Is there a veg crop you'd like to try for the first time, or a flower you've never got around to sowing or growing? The chances are that there's still time to do it. So many gardening tasks are doable in April, not restricted by it being the 'wrong time of year'. Perennial plants can be moved and divided. Roses, shrubs, trees and fruit can be planted without fear of immediate stress. The seeds of annual flowers and vegetables can be sown. The only thing to be wary of is the impulse to plant tender shrubs or seedlings out in the garden. April frosts and snow showers are a reminder that this task is still a few weeks away.

❧ SUNRISE AND SUNSET 2025 ❧

Location	Date	Rise	Set
Belfast			
	Apr 01 (Tue)	05:55 BST	19:00 BST
	Apr 11 (Fri)	05:30 BST	19:19 BST
	Apr 21 (Mon)	05:06 BST	19:38 BST
	Apr 30 (Wed)	04:46 BST	19:56 BST
Cardiff			
	Apr 01 (Tue)	05:47 BST	18:46 BST
	Apr 11 (Fri)	05:25 BST	19:03 BST
	Apr 21 (Mon)	05:04 BST	19:19 BST
	Apr 30 (Wed)	04:46 BST	19:34 BST
Edinburgh			
	Apr 01 (Tue)	05:42 BST	18:51 BST
	Apr 11 (Fri)	05:17 BST	19:11 BST
	Apr 21 (Mon)	04:52 BST	19:32 BST
	Apr 30 (Wed)	04:30 BST	19:50 BST
London			
	Apr 01 (Tue)	05:35 BST	18:34 BST
	Apr 11 (Fri)	05:13 BST	18:50 BST
	Apr 21 (Mon)	04:51 BST	19:07 BST
	Apr 30 (Wed)	04:33 BST	19:22 BST

A

❧ WEATHER CHARTS ❧

April averages 1991–2020

Location		
Belfast	Max temperature (°C)	12.84
	Min temperature (°C)	4.72
	Days of air frost (days)	1.34
	Sunshine (hours)	157.08
	Rainfall (mm)	60.35
	Days of rainfall ≥1 mm (days)	11.27
Cardiff	Max temperature (°C)	14.35
	Min temperature (°C)	5.73
	Days of air frost (days)	1.40
	Sunshine (hours)	176.98
	Rainfall (mm)	72.07
	Days of rainfall ≥1 mm (days)	10.73
Edinburgh	Max temperature (°C)	12.15
	Min temperature (°C)	4.70
	Days of air frost (days)	1.70
	Sunshine (hours)	157.26
	Rainfall (mm)	40.76
	Days of rainfall ≥1 mm (days)	8.63
London	Max temperature (°C)	14.13
	Min temperature (°C)	5.50
	Days of air frost (days)	1.36
	Sunshine (hours)	155.24
	Rainfall (mm)	49.59
	Days of rainfall ≥1 mm (days)	9.10

⇜ TASKS ⇝

Things to start

Half-hardy annuals

This group of plants includes many popular summer
flowers, such as cosmos, zinnias, cleome, tobacco plants and
French marigolds. Not as tough as cold-tolerant sweet peas,
Californian poppies and nasturtiums (hardy annuals), the
young plants need hardening off before being planted out
at the end of May, when the risk of frost should be gone.
Half-hardy seeds can be sown direct into the soil, but to
ensure a high level of germination, indoor sowing is more
reliable. Sow in seed-sowing compost that has been kept
in the house for a couple of days to warm up. Then soak
the compost, sow the seeds in trays or pots, cover with a
layer of vermiculite (to aid water retention and aeration) and
keep at a temperature of around 20°C (68°F).

A

Potatoes

The key to successful potato growing is to manage your
expectations. If you haven't got a lot of space, don't expect
never to have to buy potatoes again. Instead, choose a variety
that suits your taste (one that's especially good for roasting,
such as 'Maris Piper', or for chipping such as 'King Edward').
Or just grow them for new potatoes. This has the advantage
of fungal disease not being a problem because the crop will
be harvested before it strikes (usually in the second half of
summer). Choose a variety such as waxy 'Charlotte' and
you'll be able to make a potato salad that money can't buy in
a supermarket, or a restaurant for that matter. You can grow
potatoes in pots 30cm (12in) wide. Just put one seed potato
on top of a 15cm (6in) layer of good quality multi-purpose

compost. Cover with a little more and water it in. Keep adding more compost as the shoots begin to grow. Harvest for new potatoes when the plants start to flower. In the ground, plant potatoes in a trench 15cm (6in) deep, spacing the tubers around 30cm (12in) apart and cover them with 5cm (2in) of soil. Keep mounding the soil up around them with a spade or garden fork as the shoots start to grow.

Things to finish

Spring cabbage
The leaves of these overwintered cabbages can be picked loose now for some fresh, nutritious steamed or stir-fried veg. They've been occupying your veg patch for a long time, so you'll likely be glad of the extra space. However, the most substantial harvest will be yours if you leave the plants to develop their tightly packed pointed heads (sometimes they are referred to as pointed cabbages), which will start to come to maturity in May.

Dividing perennials
Finish lifting and dividing summer-flowering perennials this month. Not only does it help congested clumps to bloom better, dividing also provides you with the opportunity to position plants exactly where you want them. And it also means you can grow the same plant in several different places, which will add a lovely sense of flow (as well as more colour) to your garden. How tricky the plants are to dig up will be a good indication of how difficult they will be to divide. Tightly packed monsters such as daylilies will need two digging forks inserted back-to-back into the middle

of the clump, while heucheras and perennial stachys can be easily dug up and pulled into sections by hand. Those with fibrous roots, such as hostas and agapanthus, can be chopped into sections with a spade. Here are a few guidelines for the best results:

- Divide when soil is damp rather than dry and dusty.
- Have the new planting holes ready before you lift the clump, so new divisions can be replanted immediately.
- Water in each new division as soon as it has been planted.
- If splitting plants in pots, tip out all the compost to check for vine weevil grubs (white maggots) and let the birds pick them off.

A

❧ SOMETHING TO SAVOUR ❧

Tulips

I always think of tulips as the designer clothes of the garden. Let's be honest, tulips are an indulgence, a bit 'throwaway', a tad over-the-top (depending on the variety), but oh so worth it. The growing season has only just begun and these extravagant upstarts are showing off with a range of colours and patterns that are unlikely to be outdone for the rest of the year. The tulip season (which can last six weeks if you grow early 'Purple Prince' and very late-blooming yellow and white *Tulipa tarda*) is long enough to not feel fleeting, but always leaves you wanting more!

HEAD GARDENER'S PLANT
❧ OF THE MONTH – APRIL ❧

A selection of tulips chosen by Peter Edge, Head Gardener at Cragside, Northumberland

The Victorian formal gardens at Cragside would traditionally present an exuberance of colour and the bedding tulips are a key floral event to come and see in April. We plant many of these in our spring borders and have a lot of fun planning our glorious displays. Our current favourites include the red parrot tulip 'Rococo', the unusual, spidery-bloomed *Tulip acuminata*, and cream-and-yellow 'Angel's Wish'.

After the cold winter we all need colour to wake us up to the spring, and tulips offer a variety of forms and dramatic displays. No other bedding bulbs come in such a mix of colours, shapes and textures; they are utterly stylish and provide a vibrant colour palette for around one month. They work well on their own, or they can be planted with early-flowering perennials in mixed borders.

Bedding tulips grow well in a sunny open aspect in reasonably fertile soil. If you want tulips that you can grow in a shaded site or a meadow, try bright-yellow *Tulipa sylvestris*, the wild woodland tulip, which is scented and lovely. For tulips in pots, small gardens or rockeries, choose alpine species such as yellow-and-white *Tulipa tarda*, or scarlet-flowered *Tulipa linifolia*.

Though all tulips make extraordinary displays, not all of them flower year after year. To encourage future flowering, deadhead the flowers, allow the leaves to die back and offer

them a light organic feed during or after they have flowered.
Woodland tulips and alpines are more likely to naturalise
within the garden and won't need much future work.

IF YOU ONLY DO
❧ ONE THING... ❧

Protect new shoots from slugs

A

The extent to which slugs can wreak havoc on your garden
depends largely on how wet it is, and how many small
and succulent shoots are around. In a dry spring you may
forget about them completely. In a wet one you may feel
like putting a picture of a slug on a dartboard and peppering
it with holes – the same as they've done to your hostas.
Prioritising the most vulnerable growth is a good place to
start. There are many suggested slug-busting barriers, but
little scientific proof in favour of them, though there are
things to do to help reduce the chances of them damaging
your beloved plants.

- If your soil is light, nematodes (a natural pest control) can
  be applied when temperatures are in excess of 5°C (41°F).
- Water vulnerable plants in the morning rather than
  in the evening when slugs are active.
- Leave 'decoys' such as orange skins or
  old lettuce leaves in piles to attract
  slugs away from vulnerable shoots.
- Delay planting potted perennials
  until the end of May, by which time
  they will be bigger, stronger and
  growing quickly enough to shrug
  off a slug attack.

Trivia
A slug has
approximately
27,000 microscopic
teeth.

❧ PRUNING MADE SIMPLE ❧

Calluna vulgaris

Pruning winter heathers will keep the plants compact and bushy, without an unsightly 'gap' in the middle, and as such will prolong their life. If left unpruned, the plants tend to 'flop' and have a big dead area in the middle, and they don't respond well to be being chopped back to try and rectify the problem. A simple clipping in April will keep them going strong for many years. Chop back each stem on the plant, cutting into soft, leafy growth, but make sure you don't prune back into thick, woody stems. Sharp shears make the job easy so the whole plant can be pruned with just a few cuts.

❧ RECYCLING PROJECT ❧

Recycled seed trays
Clear plastic fruit punnets with drainage holes at the bottom
are ready-made seed trays and can be used to raise a small
army of seedlings. Give them a rinse before you use them,
then you're ready to go. They ideally need to be at least 6cm
(2½cm) deep.

❧ CROP OF THE MONTH ❧

A

Asparagus
If March was mild and the start of April follows suit, this
perennial vegetable will be keenly pushing through the soil
and the first full spears can be ready to cut by the end of
the month. Perhaps asparagus feels like such a treat because
of the way it gives abundantly during a month when there
are not many other crops to harvest. If you've tried and
struggled with asparagus, have another go, giving it a very
well-drained, open and sunny position. Bare-root 'crowns'
are available to plant this month, the earlier the better. They
are best planted on a ridge in a trench dug 30cm (12in)
wide and 20cm (8in) deep, with the crown on the top of the
ridge, tips just visible at soil level and the roots splayed out
and covered with soil. Asparagus
can also be grown from seed,
sown on a sunny windowsill
at around 18°C (64°F),
with young plants ready
for planting out in summer
or autumn. It will be a few

Trivia
Asparagus spears
can grow up to
10cm (4in) in a
single day.

years before cropping though, so this is one for the patient gardener, with no plans to move.

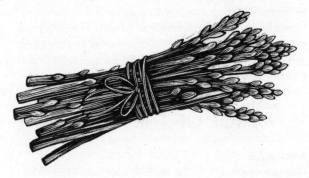

HOUSEPLANT
❧ OF THE MONTH ❧

Pelargonium 'Lady Plymouth'
There is something comforting about the scent of pelargoniums grown indoors. Walk into a porch with these plants on the ledge and there's a good chance you're about to go into a gardener's house. This minty fragranced, crinkly-leaved variety has been around more than 200 years and is one of the most refined, with its finely cut leaves, soft green with a cream edge, and delicate pink flowers. It's easy to grow – a well-lit, frost-free place being sufficient. It has good tolerance of sun and drought. Just push your finger into the compost occasionally and water when it is dry all the way down.

❧ HOW TO HELP WILDLIFE ❧

Grow some ivy

It may be that this plant feels more like a pest for you,
needing regular trimming back or yanking off brick walls
that it clings to like glue. But a mature ivy (*Hedera helix*) is
an invaluable wildlife hotspot. Its autumn flowers and winter
fruits make it a vital food source for butterflies, birds and
even bats. If you've got a mature ivy in the garden, then
you're likely to see blackbirds. If you're worried about ivy
doing damage, rest assured that it won't be responsible for
a tree dying and it doesn't have the ability to bring down a
sound, well-built wall. A good choice for growing in shade, it
will also grow well in full sun too.

*'In the spring I have counted one hundred
and thirty-six different kinds of weather
inside of four and twenty hours.'*
– Mark Twain

❧ BIRD OF THE MONTH ❧

Pied flycatcher

A male pied flycatcher looks a little like a magpie's baby
cousin, being a bit smaller than a house sparrow, with fine
black and white plumage, while the female's colouring is
browner. Most commonly seen in the west of the UK, this

summer visitor from West Africa is fond of oak trees and will search for insects in tree trunks, arriving in this country just in time to find caterpillars to feed its young.

WILD IN THE GARDEN
❧ THIS MONTH ❧

Bluebells

The average 'day of the first bluebell' is 14 April in the UK, but whether you're in the north or the south, at some point this month you can enjoy that feeling of seeing your first gently drooping flower stem, dripping with violet-blue blooms. Bluebells seem to appear almost overnight, from nowhere, but whether you are admiring a few popping up in your flower beds, or seeing hundreds of thousands of them on the woodland floor before the tree canopy closes up, this initial glimpse of their beauty is a sure sign that spring is well and truly with us.

> *Trivia*
> *Almost half of the world's bluebells are found in the UK.*

ANNUAL EVENTS AND
❧ HIGHLIGHTS ❧

Easter trails

The Easter holidays are a great opportunity to get children engaging with nature. Join a trail or egg hunt through one of the National Trust gardens and be rewarded with an Easter treat. Discover some weird and wonderful egg-laying creatures as you explore the gardens of Scotney Castle, Kent, or head to Claydon House, Buckinghamshire, to take part in an Easter trail full of sports and games. Most National Trust Easter events run for the duration of the school holidays, lasting into April.

Tulip season

Make the most of these glorious spring flowers by visiting a National Trust garden that's full of them. It's a great way to discover new varieties and get ideas for colour schemes to try at home. The Victorian Sunken Garden at Castle Ward, County Down, is home to a display of 3,500 tulips, while at Emmetts Garden, Kent, 7,000 late-flowering tulips add dazzling colour to the Cherry Avenue, using a colour scheme that dates back to 1910.

Earth Day, 22 April

Founded in 1970, Earth Day is a time to further highlight environmental concerns, with events up and down the country, from renovating local green spaces to teaching children to make their own recycled plant pots. The date was chosen in part because of the observation of Arbor Day in the US: there the 22 April is a day dedicated to planting trees.

National Asparagus Day, 23 April

As leeks and St David's Day go together, how about asparagus and St George's Day? In the Vale of Evesham, 23 April has been designated as the day the asparagus season kicks off, a hotbed of asparagus-growing, with the traditional last day of cutting being the summer solstice in June.

Harrogate Spring Flower Show, 24–27 April

Arguably the first major event in the garden show calendar, this one held at the Great Yorkshire Showground is an exciting way to mark the arrival of spring, with spectacular exhibits from florists and nurseries, and show gardens. Visit the pretty spa town afterwards, where you will see a whole host of trees adorned in beautiful spring blossom.

❧ GARDENER'S CHECKLIST ❧

☐ Take cuttings from new growth at the base of delphiniums, lupins and phlox.

☐ Plant out autumn-sown sweet peas into a sunny spot.

☐ Plant gladioli corms in well-drained soil in full sun.

☐ Start a crop of onions and shallots by planting sets, avoiding soil where you've planted them in the past two years.

☐ Sow sweetcorn in pots or trays kept in a propagator on a sunny windowsill.

☐ Remove weeds then mulch the soil around the base of fruit trees.

YOUR NOTES FOR
❧ APRIL ❧

To sow

To plant

In flower

Wildlife spotted

A

Nettles

May

'The older I grow, the more do I love spring
and spring flowers. Is it not so with you?'
– Emily Dickinson

In May it feels as if both gardens and gardeners are adorned with a youthful glow. Evenings spent sowing, potting, planting, then rewarding yourself with a drink on the patio, are light years away from the hunkering down of winter. Everything seems to have a softness and vitality, as if nothing could possibly go wrong. The joy and optimism of being in the garden in spring is contagious and a natural pick-me-up that money can't buy. At some point this month, there's a glorious moment when spring seems to become summer. It's not announced or due to any one thing in particular, it's just a special feeling that hits you – and one to breathe in and truly savour.

❧ SUNRISE AND SUNSET 2025 ❧

Location	Date	Rise	Set
Belfast			
	May 01 (Thu)	04:44 BST	19:58 BST
	May 11 (Sun)	04:24 BST	20:16 BST
	May 21 (Wed)	04:08 BST	20:33 BST
	May 31 (Sat)	03:55 BST	20:47 BST
Cardiff			
	May 01 (Thu)	04:44 BST	19:36 BST
	May 11 (Sun)	04:26 BST	19:52 BST
	May 21 (Wed)	04:12 BST	20:06 BST
	May 31 (Sat)	04:02 BST	20:19 BST
Edinburgh			
	May 01 (Thu)	04:28 BST	19:52 BST
	May 11 (Sun)	04:07 BST	20:12 BST
	May 21 (Wed)	03:49 BST	20:30 BST
	May 31 (Sat)	03:36 BST	20:45 BST
London			
	May 01 (Thu)	04:32 BST	19:24 BST
	May 11 (Sun)	04:14 BST	19:40 BST
	May 21 (Wed)	04:00 BST	19:54 BST
	May 31 (Sat)	03:49 BST	20:07 BST

M

⊱ WEATHER CHARTS ⊰

May averages 1991–2020

Location		
Belfast	Max temperature (°C)	15.74
	Min temperature (°C)	6.96
	Days of air frost (days)	0.17
	Sunshine (hours)	185.14
	Rainfall (mm)	59.63
	Days of rainfall ≥1 mm (days)	11.47
Cardiff	Max temperature (°C)	17.38
	Min temperature (°C)	8.48
	Days of air frost (days)	0.00
	Sunshine (hours)	198.37
	Rainfall (mm)	78.45
	Days of rainfall ≥1 mm (days)	11.17
Edinburgh	Max temperature (°C)	14.91
	Min temperature (°C)	7.08
	Days of air frost (days)	0.37
	Sunshine (hours)	194.66
	Rainfall (mm)	47.60
	Days of rainfall ≥1 mm (days)	9.63
London	Max temperature (°C)	17.33
	Min temperature (°C)	8.30
	Days of air frost (days)	0.03
	Sunshine (hours)	199.18
	Rainfall (mm)	50.51
	Days of rainfall ≥1 mm (days)	8.52

❧ TASKS ❧

Things to start

Sweetcorn
Sweetcorn dislikes cold so sowing this month allows for an almost seamless transition between them reaching a good size and the weather being warm enough for them to be planted out. Put two seeds into an 8cm (3in) pot, around 3cm (1¼in) deep, and cover them with sieved compost. Keep in a well-lit place at 20°C (68°F), then transplant each grass-like seedling into its own 8cm (3in) pot when it is about 10cm (4in) tall. By the time the seeds have germinated, been transplanted and had a week or two to settle into their own pots indoors, the risk of frost should have passed. Keep an eye on the weather forecast and plant them out in a mild spell.

'May is mayhem for vegetable growers. So much stuff needs to be sown.'
– Anna Pavord

Bedding plants
After what can seem like years of waiting, during which time you've been sowing, transplanting, potting and hardening off, it's finally time to plant out tender annuals and perennials that will flower through summer. Resisting the urge to plant is hard, but it will pay off if you hold your nerve and wait until the end of the month. Not only will it

be very unlikely that there is a frost, you will also have much bigger plants than if you had risked planting earlier. These will create more of an instant gap-filler and be less appealing to slugs. Keep an eye on the weather forecast because if a few windy, stormy days are in store, then it's better to keep them in their pots where they can be moved out of harm's way for a little longer, before planting out when the weather is more settled. Seeing the leaves of summer annuals being ripped to ribbons by hailstones is hard to watch!

Things to finish

Direct sowing flowers
With the soil warming up nicely and the risk of frost receding, summer-flowering annuals, whether hardy or half-hardy, can be sown direct. It's good to get the sowing completed by the end of the month, by which time gaps in the garden will be filling up. Good labelling is key after you've scattered seed direct and covered with a fine layer of sieved soil. In my case, a label attached to a scaffolding pole would be ideal as I have a knack of walking straight across empty ground sown not a week ago! To create drifts of colour, make curvy drills (shallow channels) for sowing by using the edge of a hoe blade and sprinkle the seeds into the row. If the weather is dry and mild, use a watering can with a rose head attachment to dampen the soil after sowing, and repeat later if the soil is dusty and dry on top.

Cut-and-come-again leaves indoors
Salad leaves grown on the windowsill during winter and early spring are tremendous for lifting the spirits when gardening outdoors can be a challenge, but they are likely to be running out of steam now. If you've managed to

make three harvests from the same pot of mixed leaves, then it's time to call it a day and direct sow new batches outdoors. If you've only made one or two snippings from a pot of salad leaves, give it an organic liquid feed, watering it in at compost level, to encourage a quick and vibrant final picking.

❧ SOMETHING TO SAVOUR ❧

The final throes of spring

In May there is a beautiful balance in the garden. No plant is likely to have taken up too much space. Even the leggiest of perennials still have their elegance, new growth has a softness and a sheen, while promising crops in the veg garden have a neatness, from adolescent broad beans to feathery carrot seedlings. The freshness of the month is easily missed amid all the 'doing' but it is a special time that can slip through your fingers like sand. By June, the garden is filling fast, and by the month's end is unrecognisable compared to its May look. Take the time to pause on a sunny evening and enjoy the poise and promise of the month. It's a long time before it returns.

M

'Fast fading violets cover'd up in leaves;
And mid-May's eldest child,
The coming musk-rose, full of dewy wine,
The murmurous haunt of flies on summer eves.'
– From 'Ode to a Nightingale' by John Keats

HEAD GARDENER'S PLANT
❧ OF THE MONTH – MAY ❧

Davidia involucrata **chosen by Mike Buffin,**
Head Gardener at Mount Stewart, Co. Down

We have several specimens of this lovely Chinese tree,
commonly known as the handkerchief tree, planted around
the garden at Mount Stewart, but the most notable are off
the main drive near the gate to the Lily Wood, and those
planted around the upper woodland areas of the lake. These
are my favourites as they can be seen in the distant landscape,
while up close they are real showstoppers.

May is always a riot of colour here because there is a
breathtaking array of rhododendrons in bloom, so I am
spoilt for choice when it comes to picking just one plant.
However, the handkerchief tree is very unusual looking, with
its large, 20cm (8in) long, pure-white bracts dangling down
from small ball-like flowers. It really does look as if someone
has hung myriad paper tissues from its branches.

The handkerchief tree is best planted in a slightly acidic to
neutral, fertile soil, and because it is a woodland species, it
will benefit from being mulched with leaf litter or well-
composted bark. Mulching well when the tree is young
will help it to establish quickly. Providing a location with a
little shelter from windy weather will reduce the risk of the
delicate flowers being desiccated on windy days.

This is a large garden tree that can live for well over 100
years, so it needs plenty of space. Mature specimens can

easily grow to a height of 20m (66ft), and often produce a beautiful rounded habit.

IF YOU ONLY DO
❧ ONE THING... ❧

Keep a watch for a late frost

It's a good idea to play close attention to a weather app on your phone or watch a local weather forecast each day this month to check what the overnight temperatures are set to be. If a light ground frost is forecast, it's best to move plants in pots that are being hardened off outside to somewhere indoors as it gets dark, and delay any planting out of tender plants. Covering emerging seedlings that have been direct-sown in the soil with a layer of fleece will also prevent them from being damaged by the cold.

❧ PRUNING MADE SIMPLE ❧

Choisya ternata

These spring-flowering shrubs (also called Mexican orange blossom) are best trimmed after flowering to keep them in an attractive shape. Their glossy leaves (golden yellow if you grow 'Sundance') keep the garden looking fresh all year, so maintaining a nice shape will enhance the look of the garden, and you may also get another flush of flowers from the new growth that is stimulated by trimming. Trim back stems that have just flowered, making a cut just above a pair of leaves. Avoid cutting back into thick, old wood, unless you need to completely remove unsightly shoots that are spoiling the shape of the shrub.

❧ RECYCLING PROJECT ❧

Sow new batches of veg in emptied plant pots
If you've just planted out some potted perennials, you can
wash the pots then instantly reuse them to raise some tender
veg. Don't forget to photograph the labels of the perennials
you just planted. It's my only way of remembering the
variety names of the plants I have in my garden! Sweetcorn,
courgettes, French beans, pumpkins and runner beans can
all be sown in pots now, one seed to a 5–8cm (2–3in) pot
or two seeds to a 10–13cm (4–5in) pot, filled with multi-
purpose compost. These crops will soon catch up with those
sown earlier. Keep them indoors in a well-lit spot and then
plant out when they are sturdy and showing at least one pair
of well-developed true leaves.

❧ CROP OF THE MONTH ❧

Rocket
A little rocket goes a long way, whether in a sandwich or
garnishing a soup. The two main types are wild rocket,
which has finely cut leaves with a strong flavour and can
last for years, and the milder, more round-leaved annual
salad rocket. Sow some in semi-shade and you'll get a good
supply of fresh green growth; shade also
prevents salad rocket from flowering
too early. The flowers are edible
though, with a fiery flavour. Rocket
will grow in more or less any soil,
and I can vouch for how happy
it is growing on a stony, shallow
soil. Sow it direct into the soil now,

Trivia
*In Roman times,
rocket was thought
to be an aphrodisiac
and anaesthetic.*

making a shallow trench with a hoe and covering the seeds with 1.5cm (½in) of compost or sieved soil. When tiny seedlings have emerged, keep them well watered to stop flea beetles. Tell-tale signs of this pest are seedling leaves peppered with little holes.

HOUSEPLANT
❧ OF THE MONTH ❦

Streptocarpus

This group now includes African violets, but the plants most familiarly known as *Streptocarpus* are the rosette-forming houseplants with leaves like primroses. Hailing from the Drakensberg mountains of South Africa, they have the common name of Cape primroses. Growing in the wild in woodland, placing them in a well-lit spot in the house but away from strong sunshine will suit their needs. Let the compost dry out and water gently rather than soaking the plants. Empty plant saucers a couple of minutes after watering to avoid the roots sitting in water.

❧ HOW TO HELP WILDLIFE ❧

Make a shelter for frogs and toads
You don't have to have a pond for frogs and toads to visit the garden, especially if you've got a ready-made shelter for them.

- Start by digging out a round hole around 45cm (18in) deep and 1m (3¼ft) wide. Firm the soil in the base of it with your foot.
- Fill the hole with twigs, tree prunings and logs.
- Stack pieces of lifted turf and leaf debris over the top but leave holes around the edge to allow the frogs and toads to enter easily.

❧ BIRD OF THE MONTH ❧

Whitethroat
This warbler, similar in size to the great tit, has a long tail and a soothing chirrup. A migrant from sub-Saharan Africa and Asia, it likes to forage in low scrub, and can often be seen in hedgerows in rural areas. Males – with a grey head and the white throat from which they get their name – can be seen perching on the top of hedgerow plants while in full chorus. Females have a brown head and will lay four or five eggs from May to July.

M

WILD IN THE GARDEN ❧ THIS MONTH ❧

Mayflies

Look out for this short-lived insect on the wing around ponds this month. Despite their name, adults can be seen from now until September, with delicate, lacy wings held upright, closed over their backs. Adults will keep hatching through summer, their lives no more than a matter of hours, dying once they have mated.

ANNUAL EVENTS AND
❧ HIGHLIGHTS ❧

Malvern Spring Festival, 8–11 May
This festival, held at the Three Counties Showground, Malvern, features exceptional displays of spring plants by leading nurseries, gardening talks and demonstrations by well-known gardeners and chefs, as well as lots of opportunities to buy plants and local artisan crafts.

RHS Chelsea Flower Show, 20–24 May
A celebration of woodland and the importance of water management were two hot topics in the show gardens at Chelsea in 2024. The floral marquee, filled with the most exquisite and lovingly grown plants, is a chance to expand your planting wish list and discover new gems.

National Children's Gardening Week, 24 May–1 June
Gardening with children can be a challenge but also incredibly rewarding; just be prepared for the place to be a bit messier while they help you sow or pot up plants. Time spent in the garden showing children how to grow is a massive investment in their lives that cannot be underestimated and makes many fond memories, too.

Water Saving Week, 26–30 May
Dry summers are an acute reminder of how precious water is and this week is a chance to engage with the different

ways of saving water in the garden, from recycling bath water to placing saucers underneath large containers before watering them.

National BBQ Week, 26 May–1 June
With long evenings and warm nights, this is the perfect time to start making the most of your BBQ and host some alfresco dining in the garden, garnished with freshly picked salad and herbs. Try adding a few spring onions and radishes from the garden to your barbequed food to give it a super-fresh tasty kick.

M

British Tomato Fortnight, 26 May–8 June
A well-timed reminder to either plant out your tomatoes, buy some plants, water and feed the ones that are already in place, or to get the greenhouse in shape for putting them into their final locations.

'If you focus too much on the harvest, you lose the profound meaning found in the present.'
– Miki Sakamoto

❧ GARDENER'S CHECKLIST ❧

☐ Build up the soil around the foliage of potatoes, so the tubers aren't exposed to light.

☐ Harden off seedlings and young plants in a cold frame, or in trays and boxes kept in a sheltered corner.

☐ Divide congested clumps of herbaceous perennials and replant the new divisions straight away.

☐ Direct sow carrots, beetroot and parsnips into the soil, sowing thinly along weed- and stone-free rows.

☐ Place straw beneath strawberry plants to cushion the fruit.

☐ Harvest thick, healthy rhubarb stems by giving them a sharp pull from the base.

YOUR NOTES FOR
❧ MAY ❧

To sow

_____

_____

_____

_____

_____

To plant

_____

_____

_____

_____

_____

In flower

_____

_____

_____

_____

_____

Wildlife spotted

_____

_____

_____

_____

_____

M

Long-tailed tit

June

'It is a pity June does not
last twice as long.'
– Rosemary Verey

There is a real satisfaction when early promise starts to turn into results. This begins to happen in June, something of a transition month. It will hit you at some point that potential is starting to be fulfilled. Perhaps it's seeing the tantalising orange glow of the top of a carrot, or the first fattening pea pod, or the initial flush of roses. Look back at a picture of the garden in June in September and you will be amazed at how pristine it looked, as if someone had coated every flower and leaf in glycerine. While days are still getting longer, plants are growing fast and there can be a lot to do in the garden. But the most important thing to do this month is to take time to sit, soak in the atmosphere, and *enjoy* it.

❧ SUNRISE AND SUNSET 2025 ❧

Location	Date	Rise	Set
Belfast			
	Jun 01 (Sun)	03:54 BST	20:49 BST
	Jun 11 (Wed)	03:48 BST	20:59 BST
	Jun 21 (Sat)	03:47 BST	21:03 BST
	Jun 30 (Mon)	03:51 BST	21:03 BST
Cardiff			
	Jun 01 (Sun)	04:01 BST	20:20 BST
	Jun 11 (Wed)	03:55 BST	20:29 BST
	Jun 21 (Sat)	03:55 BST	20:33 BST
	Jun 30 (Mon)	03:59 BST	20:33 BST
Edinburgh			
	Jun 01 (Sun)	03:34 BST	20:47 BST
	Jun 11 (Wed)	03:27 BST	20:57 BST
	Jun 21 (Sat)	03:26 BST	21:02 BST
	Jun 30 (Mon)	03:30 BST	21:01 BST
London			
	Jun 01 (Sun)	03:48 BST	20:08 BST
	Jun 11 (Wed)	03:43 BST	20:17 BST
	Jun 21 (Sat)	03:43 BST	20:21 BST
	Jun 30 (Mon)	03:47 BST	20:21 BST

J

❧ WEATHER CHARTS ❧

June averages 1991–2020

Location

Belfast	Max temperature (°C)	18.19
	Min temperature (°C)	9.72
	Days of air frost (days)	0.00
	Sunshine (hours)	151.09
	Rainfall (mm)	68.95
	Days of rainfall ≥1 mm (days)	11.44
Cardiff	Max temperature (°C)	20.07
	Min temperature (°C)	11.27
	Days of air frost (days)	0.00
	Sunshine (hours)	195.21
	Rainfall (mm)	73.54
	Days of rainfall ≥1 mm (days)	10.37
Edinburgh	Max temperature (°C)	17.43
	Min temperature (°C)	9.93
	Days of air frost (days)	0.00
	Sunshine (hours)	161.81
	Rainfall (mm)	66.21
	Days of rainfall ≥1 mm (days)	10.40
London	Max temperature (°C)	20.38
	Min temperature (°C)	11.17
	Days of air frost (days)	0.00
	Sunshine (hours)	193.67
	Rainfall (mm)	58.45
	Days of rainfall ≥1 mm (days)	8.73

❧ TASKS ❧

Things to start

Second batches of veg

A little like planting spring bulbs in autumn, this is a task that falls into the 'If I don't do it now I'll regret it later' category. While the first sowings of peas, beans, courgettes and salad leaves tend to be carried out amid the excitement of the arrival of spring, doing subsequent sowings can be harder to remember. Once we have a squad of young veg to tend, it's easy to spend all the time thinking about these crops and to forget that starting off even more will ensure a steady, gap-free harvest. If you've got space, sow an extra row of peas, rocket, lettuce, radishes, or pop a couple of courgette seeds into an 8cm (3in) pot of multi-purpose compost and keep on a sunny windowsill.

J

Exotic containers

We haven't all got space for bananas and tree ferns, but a little exotic haven can be easily created in a large pot. A container 45cm (18in) wide is best, so you can cram in a lot of plants. *Ensete*, *Ricinus*, *Fatsia* or *Colocasia* will make good foliage centrepieces, while calibrachoas, spider plants, sedums or creeping Jenny (*Lysimachia*) are good high-impact trailing plants. You could also squeeze in some bright celosias or dahlias to fill in gaps in the middle. Add controlled-release plant food pellets to the compost (use equal parts multi-purpose and soil-based John Innes compost) to provide food for the rest of the growing season. Place the pot in a sheltered corner that receives at least four hours of sun a day.

Things to finish

Broad beans
When you decide to harvest broad beans may depend on
whether you are a traditionalist or a bit of a foody. Do
you like to get your teeth into a thick, fleshy coated bean
that takes a bit of chewing? Or do you grow them for the
small, shiny pea-green capsules hidden inside the coat of a
still slender bean? Or perhaps you prefer them when they
are very young, like a mangetout pea? Either way, pulling
these pods is a real early summer treat. If ever there was a
vegetable to remind me not to judge by appearances, it is
the broad bean. The leathery, sometimes blotchy skins don't
exactly shout 'gourmet', but as you push your fingers along
the seam of the pod, the beautiful furry insides and fresh
beans look and smell special. I always think of these beans
as being stored inside woolly sleeping bags, or like precious
jewellery that is carefully cushioned to avoid damage. Don't
forget that if they are blackfly-free you can harvest the leafy
shoot tips at the top of the plant too and add them to a stir-
fry or salad.

Garlic

Cloves planted in autumn will be showing you that they are ready, most likely towards the end of this month, as the foliage begins to turn yellow and starts to flop. Choose a dry day with dry conditions underfoot. This will make cleaning the bulbs easier. Carefully dig down into the soil with a fork to harvest the bulbs. It's best not to push the fork in too close to the crop, to make sure you don't damage the bulbs. With the soil loosened, pull the foliage to uproot the plants and brush off loose soil. Put them on trays and leave them in a shed or on a sunny windowsill to dry out before storing in a cool place at 5–10°C (41–50°F).

❧ SOMETHING TO SAVOUR ❧

J

Warm evenings

Do we really need to be told to sit outside in the garden in midsummer? Isn't it an obvious thing to do? Well, yes and no. Or maybe I'm the only gardener that is much better at busying themselves than actually enjoying relaxing in the garden. Yes, there may be a long list of jobs to complete, but if the evening is sunny, find the time to pause and take five minutes to enjoy the warmth and the sights and sounds of the garden. Okay, we may have noisy neighbours or loud, excitable children or grandchildren, but there is something powerful in taking a pause when the garden is unveiling its full summer glory, even if life around you continues to be frenetic. The garden is the constant amid the frenzy of life and stopping to appreciate it can give us a fresh perspective.

HEAD GARDENER'S PLANT
❧ OF THE MONTH – JUNE ❧

Rosa 'Gloire de Dijon' chosen by David Swanton, Head
Gardener at Powis Castle, Powys

We grow lots of roses at Powis in beds and on walls; this
one is trained by winding it around the pillars outside the
17th-century Orangery. I like the way you can get up close
and personal with the flowers.

It is a repeat-flowering rose and flowers all through the
summer months. It has a strong fruity fragrance; the buff-
yellow flowers are globular and cupped when opening, and
later flat.

It will grow in most soil types, but as with all roses, apply
a generous layer of mulch in the spring. Our garden faces
south-east and the rose thrives in this position, never failing
to put on a beautiful display.

Prune and tie in new shoots in December, while the stems
are still flexible, removing and clearing leaves to reduce
blackspot the following year. Use an organic spray on the
leaves during the growing season – we get excellent results
using a mix of seaweed and garlic. Deadhead regularly to
encourage repeat flowering.

IF YOU ONLY DO
❧ ONE THING... ❧

Pinch out tomato sideshoots

This is one of those jobs that if you counted how many times you did it in one year you'd wonder how you ever found the time to do anything else. Or maybe you'd question whether it might be better to grow bush tomatoes, which need no pinching out. But keep going, nipping out those shoots that grow in between the main stem and each sideshoot. If the shoots are a decent size – around 8cm (3in) tall – you can root them in a glass of lukewarm water on a well-lit windowsill, then pot them up for some bonus plants.

❧ PRUNING MADE SIMPLE ❧

Topiary trimming

Topiary will start to look a bit 'frothy' this month, as new growth softens the hard edges. Oil and sharpen shears before you start, and wash and disinfect the blades in between trimming each plant to help prevent the spread of disease. You may need to soak the blades in a bucket of hot, soapy water before you start if there is dried sap stuck to them. You may trust your eye for creating the straightest line/ elephant's trunk/peacock's tail (insert here whatever crazy topiary idea you might have!) but otherwise use string tied to bamboo

J

Trivia
The National Trust garden at Knightshayes Court in Devon is famous for its topiary yew depicting seven hounds pursuing a fox.

canes inserted into the soil to give you a cutting guide. Place
a decorating sheet or tarpaulin beneath the plants you are
trimming, to make tidying up the trimmings easier. And do
check for any signs of nesting birds before you start.

৵ RECYCLING PROJECT ৵

Use corks as cane-toppers

If you've got a lot of spare corks at home, they make very
useful cane toppers. They've even already got a pilot hole
through the middle to help you push them onto the top
of the cane! Use a screwdriver to make the holes wider if
necessary and cover all your sharp cane tops to prevent any
accidents. You could also use a permanent marker to write
plant names or dates on the cork if the canes are marking an
area of seeds that have just been sown.

CROP OF THE MONTH

First early potatoes

Every year I see early potatoes come into flower and say to myself 'Is it that time already?' Because early potatoes are planted around Easter time, their entire life cycle happens just when the gardening year gets busy. There's no anxious waiting for months for something to happen. No sooner have they been planted than it's time to dig them up. And what a harvest! The taste of a freshly dug new potato is virtually impossible to replicate with anything bought in a shop, if you dig them up, scrape them and put them straight into boiling water. It's worth sacrificing size for taste and if space is limited, then just growing new potatoes makes a lot of sense. Harvesting from the end of this month means that the crop is finished before blight gets a chance to ruin the tubers, and you've got all that space ready to start something else. Loosen the soil at the base of the plant with a fork and have a rummage around to see how big the tubers are. If they are still tiny, give the plants a good soak, add some general liquid plant food, and leave the crop for another couple of weeks. When you harvest, it's best not to put your fork into the ground too close to the plant or you could end up skewering the tubers.

J

> *'All things rejoiced beneath the sun; the weeds,*
> *The river, and the cornfields, and the reeds;*
> *The willow leaves that glanced in the light breeze,*
> *And the firm foliage of the larger trees.'*
> – From 'Summer and Winter'
> by Percy Bysshe Shelley

HOUSEPLANT
❧ OF THE MONTH ❧

Philodendron scandens

This is a great plant to grow in a hanging planter and hang on a hook so that its sprawling stems can wander free and create silhouettes against your house walls. It will also work well in a simple pot placed on a shelf, but you may need to attach the pot securely to the shelf so it doesn't tip forward under the weight of the stems. It grows best in a reasonably well-lit place. It's just best to avoid direct sunlight and dark rooms that receive no natural light at all. Water each time the compost dries out and give it half-strength liquid houseplant food every couple of weeks in spring and summer.

Trivia
Perhaps Philodendron is a houseplant for tree-huggers: the first part of the name comes from the Greek word philo meaning 'love' and the second dendron meaning 'tree'.

❧ HOW TO HELP WILDLIFE ❧

Leave some stinging nettles

I seemed to spend an inordinate amount of my childhood
nursing nettle stings with dock leaves, often placed inside
my socks after the latest football/cricket-related stinging.
Had I been told at the time that these plants were important
for wildlife and also a nutritious food source I still think I
would have been all in favour of
their removal! If you can see
beyond their ability to sting,
they will become a firm
garden favourite, although
if you have small children
the plants are best
nurtured in an unused
corner rather than
a main thoroughfare.
Leaving a patch will
provide food for butterflies
and aphids (which in turn
provide food for birds and
ladybirds); in fact, nettles are a food
source for more than 40 species of insect.
Nettles also have a long history of medicinal use, and as well
as being used for nettle tea, the leaves can be cooked as a
substitute for spinach.

Trivia
*The World Nettle Eating
Competition is a Dorset
tradition. Contestants
have half an hour to
eat nettle leaves from
stalks, with the person
eating the leaves from the
longest stalk declared
the winner.*

J

❧ BIRD OF THE MONTH ❧

Long-tailed tit

A noisy bird for one so small (weighing around 8g/¼oz),
with a high-pitched chirrup, long-tailed tits will be foraging

in hedges for insects this month, moving around with their quirky bouncing flight. Both male and female look alike: they have white heads with a black stripe at the top, dark tails and blushed pink breasts, and the female will lay a single clutch of eggs in a season.

WILD IN THE GARDEN
❧ THIS MONTH ❦

Fox-and-cubs

This perennial wild flower (*Pilosella aurantiaca*) displays perhaps the finest orange colouring of any garden plant in summer. The deep orange blooms, with a yellow centre, are carried on thin, gangly stems that rise out of a hairy, ground-hugging rosette of leaves. It is so easy to casually hoe off these unpromising-looking, unasked-for plants, but so joyous to have them in full flower in summer. This is a meadow plant, thriving in damp, sunny places, but also a tough cookie. I've had them in full flower growing in little patches of soil in the cracks at the top of an old concrete step. The 'fox' refers to the fully open blooms and the 'cubs' are the flower buds that will appear alongside them this month.

ANNUAL EVENTS AND
❧ HIGHLIGHTS ❦

Bord Bia Bloom 29 May–2 June

Ireland's largest garden festival takes over Phoenix Park, Dublin for the June Bank Holiday weekend, with flowers, food and fun for all the family. The festival features show gardens, small postcard gardens, and a garden stage where experts offer advice on how to improve your plot.

BBC Gardeners' World Live, 12–15 June
A chance to get a little closer to the famous gardening TV show, with live talks by the show presenters, as well as show gardens, a floral marquee and plants for sale from a wide range of nurseries.

Rose Awareness Week, 16–22 June
A week to highlight the garden versatility of roses, with the chance to discover the best garden roses to grow and information on how to get the best results. Many National Trust gardens have fine collections of roses. The Italianate terraces at Bodnant Garden, Conwy, are packed with bed after bed of vibrant rose bushes.

Blenheim Palace Flower Show, 20–22 June
The centrepiece of the show is the Grand Floral Pavilion, full of inspiring displays from specialist plant nurseries, plus Floral Street, where exhibitors display their plants in a unique way.

J

'Plants, like people, have their preferences and don't like being thrust into the nearest available hole.'
– Beth Chatto

❧ GARDENER'S CHECKLIST ❧

☐ Put out hanging baskets in their final positions.

☐ Keep hoeing in between plants, ideally on dry, sunny days.

☐ Harvest radishes before they get gnarled and woody.

☐ Tie sweet peas to their supports using soft string.

☐ Water and feed bedding plants and annuals in containers.

☐ Thin out congested fruits on gooseberry bushes, removing pea-sized fruits.

YOUR NOTES FOR
❧ JUNE ❧

To sow

To plant

In flower

Wildlife spotted

J

Blackcurrants

July

*'A garden is to be enjoyed, and
should satisfy the mind and not only
the eye of the beholder.'*
– Penelope Hobhouse

It's easy to have your hands full in July – maybe with strawberries or lettuce leaves, or trugs of dandelions and thistles if you've been busy weeding. It is a month of abundance: there are blooms aplenty, herbs pumping out scent and luscious growth, and soft fruits are fattening nicely. With so much to gather, and enjoy looking at, it's easy to not do much in the way of gardening in July, other than harvesting and weeding. But there's still time to sow some veg for a later harvest so that you don't have to go abruptly from feast to famine. Finding a few minutes on a cool evening to scatter more seeds is well worth doing.

∻ SUNRISE AND SUNSET 2025 ∻

Location	Date	Rise	Set
Belfast			
	Jul 01 (Tue)	03:52 BST	21:02 BST
	Jul 11 (Fri)	04:02 BST	20:55 BST
	Jul 21 (Mon)	04:16 BST	20:42 BST
	Jul 31 (Thu)	04:33 BST	20:25 BST
Cardiff			
	Jul 01 (Tue)	04:00 BST	20:32 BST
	Jul 11 (Fri)	04:09 BST	20:26 BST
	Jul 21 (Mon)	04:21 BST	20:16 BST
	Jul 31 (Thu)	04:35 BST	20:01 BST
Edinburgh			
	Jul 01 (Tue)	03:31 BST	21:01 BST
	Jul 11 (Fri)	03:42 BST	20:53 BST
	Jul 21 (Mon)	03:57 BST	20:39 BST
	Jul 31 (Thu)	04:15 BST	20:21 BST
London			
	Jul 01 (Tue)	03:47 BST	20:20 BST
	Jul 11 (Fri)	03:56 BST	20:14 BST
	Jul 21 (Mon)	04:08 BST	20:04 BST
	Jul 31 (Thu)	04:23 BST	19:49 BST

J

❧ WEATHER CHARTS ❧

July averages 1991–2020

Location

Belfast	Max temperature (°C)	19.73
	Min temperature (°C)	11.56
	Days of air frost (days)	0.00
	Sunshine (hours)	146.31
	Rainfall (mm)	73.62
	Days of rainfall ≥1 mm (days)	13.00
Cardiff	Max temperature (°C)	21.79
	Min temperature (°C)	13.12
	Days of air frost (days)	0.00
	Sunshine (hours)	199.56
	Rainfall (mm)	83.58
	Days of rainfall ≥1 mm (days)	11.23
Edinburgh	Max temperature (°C)	19.29
	Min temperature (°C)	11.60
	Days of air frost (days)	0.00
	Sunshine (hours)	169.93
	Rainfall (mm)	72.06
	Days of rainfall ≥1 mm (days)	11.47
London	Max temperature (°C)	22.73
	Min temperature (°C)	13.34
	Days of air frost (days)	0.00
	Sunshine (hours)	199.79
	Rainfall (mm)	50.49
	Days of rainfall ≥1 mm (days)	8.43

❧ TASKS ❧

Things to start

Houseplant holidays

One of the easiest ways to turn your patio into a rich, leafy tropical paradise is to move all your potted houseplants onto it. Not only will it enhance your outdoor living, it will also expose your plants to higher levels of humidity and rainfall. Whatever houseplant you are bringing outdoors, start by keeping them in a shady corner for a few days, so they can adjust to the new light levels. Where you keep them on the patio will depend on their individual growing needs, but wait until the outdoor temperatures are no lower than 12°C (54°F) and if colder spells or storms are forecast, bring them back indoors.

Things to finish

J

Blackcurrants

While summer fruits are perhaps most associated with sweetness, along comes the antioxidant-packed blackcurrant to add a sharper tone. I can't get enough of these fruits that put the 'tart' into a fruit tart!

The most underrated aspect of blackcurrants has to be their scent: a delicious warm aroma of leaves and fruit that makes harvesting them another landmark moment of the summer garden. Carefully pick them off by hand or – if all the

Trivia
Around 90 per cent of Britain's blackcurrant crop is used to make a very popular brand of blackcurrant cordial. That's about 10,000 tonnes of blackcurrants!

fruits on a bunch (sometimes called a strig) are ripe – simply snip off the whole bunch. When you get them indoors you can carefully use a kitchen fork to remove the fruit from the stalks.

Trimming hardy geraniums

With so many plants and crops jostling to take centre stage this month, it's easy to overlook those that have faded, and forget that they were ever there. At the start of the month, remember your hardy geraniums. Flowers are likely to be sparse and if the foliage is looking tired, take out some garden shears and cut it back to just above ground level. You'll soon be rewarded with fresh, spring-like foliage to freshen up your borders, and maybe some more flowers too.

❧ SOMETHING TO SAVOUR ❦

Strawberries

Rummaging through the strawberry patch in the morning in search of fresh fruits is a fine way to start the day (as long as you don't get prickled by a hidden bramble). Growing a mix of early, mid-season and late varieties will prolong this summer ritual. 'Honeoye' is a very early one; 'Cambridge Favourite' a classic, very sweet mid-season strawberry; and 'Malwina' is a late type with an intense flavour. Strawberry plants run out of steam after about four years so if you have a patch in its third year, and have the space, make plans to add some new plants. Then, when you dispose of your old patch next year, you'll already have established plants taking their place.

HEAD GARDENER'S PLANT
❧ OF THE MONTH – JULY ❧

Iris ensata 'Kumo-no-obi' (syn. I. *kaempferi*) chosen
by Una Quinn, Head Gardener at Hezlett House and
Downhill Demesne, Co. Londonderry

This plant is a summer highlight in the Bishopsgate Bog
Garden at Downhill Demesne. With a name that translates
from Japanese as 'band of clouds', the petals offer splashes of
marvellous colour in the balmy north-coast days of July, as
well as having a powdery soft sweet fragrance.

The multiple blossoms on strong stems last around 3–4
weeks and are used to best effect when planted *en masse*.
The petals are in three parts: the standards, the stigma flaps
and the falls. The petals have basal yellow lines with a purple
outer perianth. The fans of leaves look like Samurai swords
and soak up the summer sunshine. *Iris ensata* grows well
with the UK native yellow flag iris (*I. pseudacorus*), which is
known to naturally filter pollution.

J

Phosphate is important in order for this iris to grow well,
so feed for vigour in early spring with a balanced aquatic
slow-release fertiliser. Avoid bonemeal. Remove other
competing vegetation to expose the crown of the plant to
the sun and cut back rotted foliage in winter. It prefers moist
soil/boggy conditions in part shade or sun and grows up to
90cm (3ft) tall.

IF YOU ONLY DO
❧ ONE THING... ❧

Plug gaps with summer colour
Most textbooks will advise against planting anything this month, but to someone who loves to plant, it's a bit like telling a three-year-old not to eat the marshmallow in front of them. While it's not advisable to plant something out in searing hot sun and temperatures above the high twenties Celsius (80+°F), July is a month where gaps become obvious. And on a cool, cloudy day, if you've got a gap you can fill, go for it. Annuals can keep flowering until the first frosts, and perennials such as dahlias, crocosmias or salvias in flower can make a big impact instantly, perhaps like inserting a missing piece of a jigsaw puzzle. Water well after planting and apply a mulch of compost 5cm (2in) thick around the base of the plant. Be prepared to water in dry spells afterwards. Take a walk around the garden each evening and give any new additions some water if you notice leaves drooping.

'A world without tomatoes is like a string quartet without violins.'
– Laurie Colwin

❧ PRUNING MADE SIMPLE ❧

Old-fashioned, once-flowering roses

Roses that only give one flush of flowers in summer may seem like an indulgence, but some of them create such a special display that summer would be poorer without them. Then there can also be the bonus of pretty hips and even attractive foliage if you grow blue-leaved *Rosa glauca*. Once-flowering roses are best trimmed straight after flowering to encourage more shoots to develop for next year. Cut any dead or diseased stems back to clean wood (if the wound is green all the way through then you're good), then shorten the whole plant by about one-third, and cut the outer stems back a bit further if you want to create a rounded, dome-shaped plant. It is also a good idea to remove one or two of the oldest, thickest stems if the plant is well established, cutting them off at the base. You may need loppers for this.

J

❧ RECYCLING PROJECT ❧

Broken pot succulent displays

In life, things break (if you have small children no doubt you are reminded of this often) and terracotta pots have a habit of cracking, whether it's because of cold, old age or accidents. In fact, I'm sure many of us can empathise with these clay vessels. If you've still got the fragments of a few terracotta pot mishaps, try turning them into a succulent centrepiece.

Add gritty compost to the largest piece of broken pot (ideally a piece that has the base intact). Then insert pot fragments firmly into the compost, and plant succulents into the gaps. Finish it off by watering in the plants then covering the compost surface with gravel or small stone chippings.

❧ CROP OF THE MONTH ❧

Kohlrabi

If you're looking for a new crop to grow from seed this month and want to try something that isn't leafy, then give this quirky brassica a go. It forms a swollen base, like a colourful tennis ball, with leaf stalks attached to it. With a taste similar to turnip, it can be chopped and roasted, or grated and used in a homemade coleslaw.

Sow the seed thinly along shallow drills made with the edge of a hoe blade, around 1cm (½in) deep. Choose a patch of soil that is slow to dry out and hasn't had manure added to it. Cover the seeds with sieved soil then water gently.

Thin out the seedlings when they have true leaves, to leave a final spacing of one plant every 15cm (6in) along the row. Keep the young plants well watered so the soil is never dry and dusty; water in the morning to reduce slug damage.

Keep weeding around the crop and mulch with compost after watering to keep the soil cool and damp during hot spells. Harvest when the roots are about the size of a tennis ball. Leaf stalks can be harvested too and lightly steamed.

J

'*Above all my policy is to be adventurous and have fun. It does not matter if plans do not always work out. It's gardening; it goes on and on.*'
– Carol Klein

HOUSEPLANT
❧ OF THE MONTH ❦

Zamioculcas zamiifolia

Perhaps unsurprisingly known as the 'ZZ plant', this is one of the best houseplants for beginners – or non-beginners with a hefty portfolio of houseplants that they have successfully managed to coax to a premature end. From shady forests and stony terrain in East Africa, it has fleshy roots that can store water for long periods. Its attractive, deep-green, shield-shaped leaves contain high levels of water, and the plant can tolerate low light levels, as well as a couple of weeks without water. Just avoid exposure to direct sun, keep at a temperature of 15–26°C (59–79°F) and mist the plant occasionally in winter to raise humidity. Growing up to 1m (3¼ft) tall, it's an ideal evergreen for adding interest to an awkward dark corner in a room.

❧ HOW TO HELP WILDLIFE ❦

Give birds water

If you don't have a pond in your garden, leave out a shallow tray of water for birds to drink from, to keep them hydrated in hot, dry spells. Or add a bird bath if you don't have one. Place it a couple of metres (around 6ft) from an area of trees or shrubs so the birds have some shelter to easily move to if necessary. Clean the bath with a weak solution of disinfectant every couple of weeks, then rinse it out well.

❧ BIRD OF THE MONTH ❧

Blackbird

Is there a more melodious sound in the garden than the song of the blackbird? They are great companions to have hopping about with you while you potter in the garden. They are particularly fond of earthworms, and will listen for their movement underground. The breeding season for this familiar garden bird ends this month, with blackbirds having two or three broods. You can see blackbirds in the garden all year round, and you are very likely to have them with you in the garden if you have a lot of autumn-berried shrubs, or leave a few windfallen apples on the ground.

Trivia
The oldest blackbird on record was 21 years and one month old, way above their average life expectancy of around three years.

J

'There is immense satisfaction in the intimacy of a restricted area, where no space can be wasted, everything has to be considered, cherished, made to do its best.'
– Penelope Lively

WILD IN THE GARDEN
❧ THIS MONTH ❧

Hoverflies

With a name derived from the way they hover in mid-air, these two-winged flies are often mistaken for wasps or bees but thankfully, if you encounter one, they don't sting. Very useful to have in the garden, they are pollinators; many hoverfly species feed on aphids when they are at the larvae stage and some can also help control populations of whitefly and scale insects.

Trivia
There are more than 280 species of hoverfly in Britain.

ANNUAL EVENTS AND
❧ HIGHLIGHTS ❦

Hampton Court Garden Festival, 1–6 July
A flower show on a grand scale and one you can arrive at in style by taking a boat trip along the River Thames. Look forward to large show gardens, floral marquees, rose exhibits and an enormous range of food, drink and craft outlets. This is a big summer day out for garden and plant lovers.

Big Butterfly Count, 11 July–3 August
Help play your part in the world's biggest survey of butterflies by counting the number of butterflies that you see in 15 minutes during a spell of bright, sunny weather, either in your garden or on a walk. The results of the count, organised by the charity Butterfly Conservation, are invaluable in the fight to conserve threatened species.

J

RHS Tatton Park Flower Show, 16–20 July
Don't miss the usual inspiring mix of show gardens, floral exhibits and talented craftspeople, with live music and lots of fun for the family.

National Preserving Awareness Week, 26 July–1 August
Celebrate the art of preserving your own food this week. Fresh blackcurrants and gooseberries from the garden are a good place to start if you've got a glut of them and want to make the most of your crop.

❧ GARDENER'S CHECKLIST ❧

☐ Move plants in pots into shade on very hot days to reduce stress.

☐ Water plants early in the morning to reduce evaporation (watering at night will encourage slugs).

☐ Tie in new shoots on climbers, positioning them to fill any empty gaps.

☐ Train cucumber plants up bamboo cane supports.

☐ Feed tomatoes, chillies and peppers weekly with a potassium-rich plant food (comfrey is a good homemade option).

☐ Check peas daily for harvesting and pick pods before the peas are fat and bulky.

YOUR NOTES FOR
⮞ JULY ⮜

To sow

To plant

In flower

Wildlife spotted

J

Meadowsweet

August

'The dahlia's first duty in life is to
flaunt and to swagger and to carry
gorgeous blooms well above its leaves,
and on no account to hang its head.'
– Gertrude Jekyll

I like to think of August as the most colourful time of year in the garden. A whole host of late-flowering perennials begin to flower, to join your annuals, roses and shrubs, and they are mixed with maturing grasses. It's a spectacular month for the ornamental garden. There are fruit and vegetable crops maturing rapidly too, but if drought strikes it can be a difficult month. Surrounded by the outstanding beauty that becomes such a daily presence, it's easy to get complacent. In August a lot of plants start to tire and I think that towards the end of the month the gardener has a choice: decide to preen, prop and prolong, or let the garden go and embrace a billowing, scruffy nature. It's still a busy month and time may well be the deciding factor for which method you adopt. Both have their merits.

❧ SUNRISE AND SUNSET 2025 ❧

Location	Date	Rise	Set
Belfast			
	Aug 01 (Fri)	04:34 BST	20:24 BST
	Aug 11 (Mon)	04:52 BST	20:03 BST
	Aug 21 (Thu)	05:10 BST	19:41 BST
	Aug 31 (Sun)	05:29 BST	19:17 BST
Cardiff			
	Aug 01 (Fri)	04:36 BST	20:00 BST
	Aug 11 (Mon)	04:52 BST	19:42 BST
	Aug 21 (Thu)	05:08 BST	19:22 BST
	Aug 31 (Sun)	05:24 BST	19:00 BST
Edinburgh			
	Aug 01 (Fri)	04:17 BST	20:19 BST
	Aug 11 (Mon)	04:36 BST	19:58 BST
	Aug 21 (Thu)	04:56 BST	19:34 BST
	Aug 31 (Sun)	05:15 BST	19:09 BST
London			
	Aug 01 (Fri)	04:24 BST	19:48 BST
	Aug 11 (Mon)	04:39 BST	19:30 BST
	Aug 21 (Thu)	04:55 BST	19:10 BST
	Aug 31 (Sun)	05:11 BST	18:48 BST

A

❧ WEATHER CHARTS ❧

August averages 1991–2020

Location

Belfast	Max temperature (°C)	19.40
	Min temperature (°C)	11.47
	Days of air frost (days)	0.00
	Sunshine (hours)	141.86
	Rainfall (mm)	84.95
	Days of rainfall ≥1 mm (days)	13.52
Cardiff	Max temperature (°C)	21.43
	Min temperature (°C)	12.92
	Days of air frost (days)	0.00
	Sunshine (hours)	185.30
	Rainfall (mm)	104.82
	Days of rainfall ≥1 mm (days)	12.40
Edinburgh	Max temperature (°C)	19.07
	Min temperature (°C)	11.51
	Days of air frost (days)	0.00
	Sunshine (hours)	159.97
	Rainfall (mm)	71.57
	Days of rainfall ≥1 mm (days)	10.37
London	Max temperature (°C)	22.26
	Min temperature (°C)	13.35
	Days of air frost (days)	0.00
	Sunshine (hours)	188.25
	Rainfall (mm)	67.65
	Days of rainfall ≥1 mm (days)	9.25

❧ TASKS ❧

Things to start

Winter radishes

Sowing a salad radish might not be high on your list of
priorities in spring when, let's be honest, there are more
exciting things to be planting. But as summer enters its final
month, and most crops are in their later stages of life, it's a
bonus to be able to sow some of these fresh, crunchy veg to
harvest at the end of autumn and into winter. They tend to
be bigger than the small, pink ones grown through spring
and summer, and are slower-growing, but they will make a
very welcome addition to the kitchen in the cold months.
Sow the seed thinly on the soil surface, a raised bed or in
deep pots of multi-purpose compost. Deep, free-draining
conditions are needed for the longest, most uniform roots.
Thin the seedlings to 20cm (8in) apart.

Hardy annuals

It's not easy to fix our gaze on next year's flowers when
the garden is still showing off its summer glory, but if
you've got some spare time and spare seed trays or pots
hanging around, half an hour of sowing can give some extra
oomph to your flower garden next year. You can also sow
them direct if your soil isn't parched, or you have some
space available in a raised bed. Hardy annual flowers such as
Delphinium consolida, *Orlaya grandiflora*, *Clarkia*, *Cerinthe* and
Ammi majus can all be sown now. Keep pots or cell trays in
a sheltered spot outside. Transplant young plants from cells
into individual 8cm (3in) pots when well rooted later on
in autumn.

Things to finish

Plums

This is the fruit that I find hardest to do anything with other than eat raw, and there has to be a pretty big glut for any to make it into the freezer or even a dessert. A ripe, home-grown plum, with soft skin and sun-warmed flesh is a thing of beauty that makes those wooden, bitter ones sold in supermarkets in the winter months seem like a different fruit altogether. Give the fruits a gentle twist and they should offer no resistance to let you know they are ripe. If you've got an old tree and need a ladder to get them all, do make sure you've got someone steadying it at the bottom. If you haven't, try giving the tree a very gentle shake. A layer of fleece placed on the ground under the tree will help cushion the fruits as they fall.

Autumn-flowering bulbs

At the beginning of the month, there's just time to squeeze in some autumn-flowering bulbs. These often-overlooked plants – including autumn crocus, autumn snowflake, colchicums and autumn cyclamen (*Cyclamen hederifolium*) – will add another dimension to your garden, with some fresh and vibrant colour. Plant in parts of the garden where the soil drains well.

A

❧ SOMETHING TO SAVOUR ❧

Self-sown plants

Just how many 'stray' plants have enhanced the beauty of your garden this summer? I'm more than happy to pull out unwanted self-seeders (although more reluctant than pulling out thistles and brambles) but they still play a big part in the look of the garden. It's at this time of year that I realise how letting plants go can create a sense of flow that is often better than anything I have tried to plan or coax into being.

139

Now is a great time to take some pictures of the garden to give you an idea of what it looks like when at 'full capacity'. Then, when you see those tiny seedlings of California poppy, pot marigold or Cerinthe start to pop up, take a look at last year's garden and work out where they are best transplanted to, and which parts of the garden would benefit from less or more of a particular self-seeder.

HEAD GARDENER'S PLANT
❧ OF THE MONTH – AUGUST ❧

Lagerstroemia indica 'Red Imperator' chosen by Chris Flynn, Head Gardener at Dyffryn Gardens, Cardiff

This spectacular plant (also known as crepe myrtle) grows in the Mediterranean Garden alongside acacia, olive trees, sea hollies (*Eryngium*) and salvias. A small tree, it usually comes into flower in August, producing sprays of unusual-shaped, deep crimson flowers. It is a real stand-out in the garden this month and will become even more so in future years because a mature specimen develops the most stunning, flaking, patterned bark.

A free-draining soil on a sunny, but sheltered site is best. The Mediterranean Garden at Dyffryn offers a lot of protection from northerly winds, which can often be the most devastating, so giving it shelter is important. They can grow in partial shade as some of our collection do, but they will do best in a sunny position.

In terms of gardening, there's not a lot to do with these plants if they are growing in the right place. They will get tougher as they get older and will look after themselves. They can be quite late to come into leaf compared to other trees and may give the appearance of having died off in the spring, but be patient and have faith: they'll catch up soon enough!

IF YOU ONLY DO
❧ ONE THING... ❦

Summer-prune wisteria

Once the glorious late spring/early summer flowers of wisteria have withered, these plants will have put on lots of green growth, and now is the time to trim it back to keep it under control. Cut each green shoot formed this year back to five or six leaves from the base of the shoot. This will channel the plant's energy into producing flower buds for next year. Now is also a good time to train stray shoots back onto their supports, and if this can't be done, cut them out completely.

Trivia

The largest known wisteria in the world is a Chinese wisteria (Wisteria sinensis) growing in Sierra Madre, California, USA. It was planted in 1894, has branches measuring more than 150m (500ft) and covers an area of 0.4ha (1 acre).

A

❧ PRUNING MADE SIMPLE ❧

Lavender

Towards the end of the month, those intense purple lavender flowers that were buzzing with bees in high summer will have turned grey, indicating it's time for a tidy up. Cut back all the flowered shoots as hard as you like but not into the old, thick wood or it won't resprout readily. Make sure you are cutting into leaf growth made in this growing season and you'll be okay. This will help keep your lavender plants dense and compact and prevent them from splitting in the middle.

❧ RECYCLING PROJECT ❧

Water recycling

Water is probably the easiest resource to recycle in the garden and in the house. But it's easy not to do it too. For your houseplants, have a jug at hand for all the water that collects in saucers. This will stop your houseplants becoming waterlogged and you can then use the liquid to water plants in the garden. To save water, place a container under the tap every time you use it in the kitchen and tip the contents into a watering can. This way you'll always have a full watering can when you need it. Outside, connect your guttering to a water butt: just one spell of rainfall can result in a substantial water harvest. Leave other containers outside to collect rainwater; when you put them out, make sure they are full (or heavy) enough not to get blown over in the wind.

❧ CROP OF THE MONTH ❧

Raspberries

There are few soft fruit crops that can be picked in midsummer and also in November, but that joy can be yours if you grow summer and autumn-fruiting varieties of raspberry. It's best to grow them in separate rows or different parts of the garden, so they don't get mixed up, because they ideally require pruning at different times. Look at the plants every day for fresh fruit because it soon spoils if left on the cane a few days too long. Check the plants over well: some fruits will be hidden behind leaves. If berries haven't formed fully and crumble into lots of tiny pieces, feed and mulch in spring to give a boost of nutrients and keep plants well-watered during dry spells in spring and summer.

HOUSEPLANT
❧ OF THE MONTH ❧

A

Peace lily *(Spathiphyllum)*

Maybe it's just me but whenever I see someone interviewed from their home via videolink on the TV, there seems to be one of these plants, leaves splayed out and exhausted, dying quietly in the corner. A popular houseplant due to its reputation for purifying air, it is really quite a tolerant soul, but just not keen on a very sunny spot in direct light. At home, mine seem to thrive in a cool, poorly lit hall where they elevate an otherwise unremarkable half-moon table into a satisfyingly simple-to-look-after feature. In a shady place the leaf colour will be darker but it will flower less. For the

best display of flowers, a well-lit spot out of direct sun is ideal. Water each time the compost dries out, but only just enough to moisten it. Re-pot every few years and remove the spent flowers, snipping them off at the base of the flower stem when they start to turn brown. It's best not to try and pull them off by hand because they are far more stubborn than they appear and giving them a yank could damage the rest of the plant.

⮑ HOW TO HELP WILDLIFE ⮐

Grow lots of single flowers

There are probably more flowers on show in the garden than in any other month of the year, but if this hasn't resulted in a buzz of insect activity then it may be that you have a proliferation of 'blowsy' complicated blooms and not many simple, single flowers. The extra petals in double flowers are produced at the expense of stamens, which means that they contain little pollen; they also make it difficult for butterflies and bees to reach the nectaries at the base of the petals where they want to feed on the nectar. Add more single flowers with prominent stamens into your garden and that wonderful gentle hum of insects will become the soundtrack to your summer.

'Gardening is learning, learning, learning. That's part of the fun of it. You are always learning.'
– Dame Helen Mirren

❧ BIRD OF THE MONTH ❧

Starlings

Smaller than a blackbird, with their black feathers shining blue and green in the late summer sun, starlings will be inspecting lawns for leatherjackets, spiders and earthworms this month. Noisy birds, with a call a bit like a buzzer, most starlings spend all year in the UK but they will be

Trivia
Starlings are very good mimics and have been recorded copying the sounds of car alarms, phone ringtones and mammals, as well as putting together their own 'remixes' of the calls of other birds!

A

joined by more arriving from northern Europe next month. Starlings are sociable birds – you will increase your chances of seeing them in the garden if you put up a bird feeder.

WILD IN THE GARDEN
❧ THIS MONTH ❧

Meadowsweet

This wild flower (*Filipendula ulmaria*) is likely to be spotted if you have a ditch around the edge of your garden boundary, because it thrives in damp habitats. An upright plant with frothy clusters of sweetly scented white or creamy flowers on stilt-like stems, it is also easily identifiable by its foliage, which has prominent veins and toothed edges. Try growing this elegant plant around the margins of a pond. Its flowers are insect-friendly, and it is a food plant for several species of moth, including the emperor moth.

ANNUAL EVENTS AND
❧ HIGHLIGHTS ❧

RHS Hyde Hall Flower Show, 30 July–3 August

Take a visit to this exciting Essex garden to pick up advice from a wide range of expert plant growers; enjoy spectacular summer displays; and be entertained by talks and demonstrations in the Potting Shed Theatre.

National Allotment Week, 4–10 August
Celebrate the important role that allotments play in our communities by getting involved in a local event at a site near you. Maybe it's time to take the plunge and put yourself down on a waiting list for a new plot.

Shrewsbury Flower Show, 8–9 August
A diverse show to enjoy during the school holidays, with a wide range of vibrant floral arrangements, live music and demonstrations from expert gardeners and chefs.

Great Comp Garden Show, 9–10 August
In the beautiful garden at Great Comp, Kent, savour the summer show, featuring specialist nurseries, local artists and craftspeople, and enjoy refreshments at the Old Dairy Tearoom.

Afternoon Tea Week, 11–17 August
There are hundreds of National Trust places to unwind with a pot of tea and some tasty treats, including the Squires Pantry at Felbrigg Hall, Norfolk, where you can sit in the courtyard with your refreshments and soak up the sun.

A

Southport Flower Show, 14–17 August
There's summer holiday fun for all the family with children's entertainment, arena shows, talks, show gardens, a food village and a large amateur growers' competition that's open to everyone. Take along your best marrow or bunch of roses!

❧ GARDENER'S CHECKLIST ❧

☐ Deadhead annuals, perennials and roses to keep the flowers coming.

☐ Take cuttings of fresh new shoots on pelargoniums and keep on a sunny windowsill.

☐ Keep evergreens in pots well-watered during dry spells.

☐ Take cuttings from the soft, non-flowering shoots of herbs such as thyme, hyssop and rosemary.

☐ Plant new strawberry runners in an open, sunny site in rich soil.

☐ Remove the lower leaves from tomatoes to improve airflow and expose fruits to more light.

'Gardeners may sigh over their salvias, worship their wisterias, but soil, they take for granted.'
– Charlotte Mendelson

YOUR NOTES FOR
❧ AUGUST ❧

To sow

To plant

In flower

A

Wildlife spotted

Marrows

September

'August and September are like twins in the veg garden: both months feature similar crops, but each has its own personality.'
– Sarah Raven

I will forever associate September with harvest festivals, as I expect a lot of people raised on a farm or in rural areas will too. The main reason is the scent. Spring and midsummer scents may be the most celebrated, but there is something about the smell of freshly dug beetroot, carrots, onions and potatoes that instantly takes me back decades. It is a month of bounty, with almost every type of crop seemingly giving out something to pick. This is the month when I'm glad to have autumn- as well as summer-fruiting raspberries. As they start to colour up, it's a reminder that they will give fresh, tasty pickings right up until the first frosts. This is the last month of the year that can truly feel like summer. Daily deadheading last month will have been well rewarded by now, with more fresh annual and perennial flowers. The roses may well be having another go, too.

☙ SUNRISE AND SUNSET 2025 ☙

Location	Date	Rise	Set
Belfast			
	Sep 01 (Mon)	05:31 BST	19:14 BST
	Sep 11 (Thu)	05:49 BST	18:49 BST
	Sep 21 (Sun)	06:07 BST	18:24 BST
	Sep 30 (Tue)	06:24 BST	18:01 BST
Cardiff			
	Sep 01 (Mon)	05:25 BST	18:58 BST
	Sep 11 (Thu)	05:41 BST	18:35 BST
	Sep 21 (Sun)	05:57 BST	18:12 BST
	Sep 30 (Tue)	06:12 BST	17:52 BST
Edinburgh			
	Sep 01 (Mon)	05:17 BST	19:06 BST
	Sep 11 (Thu)	05:36 BST	18:40 BST
	Sep 21 (Sun)	05:56 BST	18:13 BST
	Sep 30 (Tue)	06:14 BST	17:50 BST
London			
	Sep 01 (Mon)	05:13 BST	18:46 BST
	Sep 11 (Thu)	05:29 BST	18:23 BST
	Sep 21 (Sun)	05:45 BST	18:00 BST
	Sep 30 (Tue)	05:59 BST	17:40 BST

S

❧ WEATHER CHARTS ❧

September averages 1991–2020

Location		
Belfast	Max temperature (°C)	17.34
	Min temperature (°C)	9.64
	Days of air frost (days)	0.00
	Sunshine (hours)	112.03
	Rainfall (mm)	69.64
	Days of rainfall ≥1 mm (days)	11.63
Cardiff	Max temperature (°C)	19.10
	Min temperature (°C)	10.70
	Days of air frost (days)	0.00
	Sunshine (hours)	151.89
	Rainfall (mm)	86.31
	Days of rainfall ≥1 mm (days)	11.8
Edinburgh	Max temperature (°C)	16.88
	Min temperature (°C)	9.65
	Days of air frost (days)	0.03
	Sunshine (hours)	130.09
	Rainfall (mm)	54.92
	Days of rainfall ≥1 mm (days)	9.93
London	Max temperature (°C)	19.13
	Min temperature (°C)	11.12
	Days of air frost (days)	0.00
	Sunshine (hours)	145.48
	Rainfall (mm)	59.08
	Days of rainfall ≥1 mm (days)	8.97

✂ TASKS ✂

Things to start

Hyacinths for winter blooms

Plant specially prepared hyacinth bulbs in pots this month
for some deliciously scented, blowsy winter blooms to cheer
up the house on dark, cold days.

- Choose shallow terracotta pots and fill them almost to the
  top with multi-purpose compost.
- Place the bulbs on the compost surface, leaving a 3cm
  (1½in) gap between each bulb so they aren't touching.
- Add more compost around the bulbs, so that they are
  half-covered.
- Place the pot somewhere cool and dark to simulate the
  plants being planted below ground.
- Check the bulbs weekly and when you see shoots, move
  them out of the dark and into an unheated greenhouse,
  porch or conservatory.
- As the flower buds begin to form, move the pot to its final
  place, ideally a cool windowsill, where the flowers will
  last much longer than in a warm, centrally-heated room.

S

Spinach

Sow a new crop of spinach now for some fresh 'last gasp'
salad leaves before the cold weather arrives. Sown direct
in the soil this month, they will provide a welcome supply
of nutritious cut-and-come-again leaves. If covered with
a cloche or grown in a polytunnel or a cold greenhouse
border, they will keep cropping until the first frost;
depending on the severity of winter, you could have new
supplies up to the end of the year. Sow the seed directly onto

the soil surface, making a shallow drill and then sprinkling the seed along it. Cover with sieved compost; water using a watering can with a rose head, and the seeds will be up in a week or so. Use barriers to protect the small seedlings from slugs and snails, and avoid watering at night, which could make them more of a problem.

Trivia
Spinach is more than 90 per cent water, making it useful for hydration. Spinach is a good source of protein, fibre, calcium, iron and folate.

Things to finish

Grapes
They say that the proof of the pudding is in the eating and this is certainly true when it comes to harvesting grapes. If you've got grapes growing in the greenhouse and you think they are ready to harvest, pick one off and try it, and then you'll know! Remove whole bunches from the plant by cutting off the main stalk, holding the bunch to the stem. If you're growing wine grapes, which won't be as sweet, they have reached ripeness when the skins are soft to the touch.

'There comes a time when autumn asks "What have you been doing all summer?"'
– Unknown

Onions
As the tops of onions flop over, almost at right angles, and begin to turn brown, they're telling you that they

don't want to play anymore and it's time to take them out. Push a fork into the soil to lift them up, then put them in trays as they are and leave them in a sunny place indoors to dry out for a couple of weeks. Or, if the weather is fine, they can stay somewhere sunny outside. Once the leaves are dry and papery, snip them off to leave a short stalk and store the onions in nets, bags or trays; keep them somewhere cool, dry and airy.

❧ SOMETHING TO SAVOUR ❧

An abundance of herbs

After a full growing season, many herbs will be a mass of pungent, tasty leaves this month, and while they might not look much from afar, close harvesting can give you a glut of produce for drying, freezing or making tea. September is a good month to make a significant harvest of deciduous herbs such as mint, lemon balm and oregano, while evergreens such as rosemary and thyme can also be given a good trim (although not into old wood) to keep them compact.

S

HEAD GARDENER'S PLANT
❧ OF THE MONTH – SEPTEMBER ❧

Salvia 'Royal Bumble', chosen by Lottie Allen, Head
Gardener at Hidcote Manor Garden, Gloucestershire

Salvia 'Royal Bumble' is a real favourite, especially if it hasn't
been checked by the preceding winter's cold. The plant
grows to around 75cm (30in) in the best conditions and we
use it as a 'front to middle' character in the Red Borders
at Hidcote, among a palette of annuals, tender perennials,
grasses and shrubs. The dark green foliage works well with
the bronze foliage of ajugas, dahlias and sedums.

I first grew it on St Michael's Mount in Cornwall, protected
by the worst of the salt winds by a walled garden. Allowed to
grow in warmer, well-drained soil, this plant flourishes and
rewards the gardener by flowering from May until October.
Even in the considerably colder and wetter climate of
Hidcote it appears to bloom from June until the hard frosts.
I love the gentle scent of sage when you brush past it and
the vibrant red flowers. We often take semi-ripe cuttings
in late summer as a precaution; however, most years the
established plants will pull through and recover, flowering
according to the next season's weather.

IF YOU ONLY DO
❧ ONE THING... ❧

Sort out brambles

Brambles are very good at impersonating other plants, as you may have discovered to your disadvantage if you've put your hand into a row of strawberries to do some picking and wondered where that sharp scratch came from. Yes, I'm speaking from painful experience! And, because they are low-lying when young, they can get lost in a packed border. Now is a good time to target them before they cause bigger problems. Choose a day after a good fall of rain, and young ones should pull out if you give them a good heave. Otherwise, use a hand fork to disturb the roots. If you've got some brambles in a scruffy corner, then you may want to leave the stems so that you can harvest fruit from them next year, but only if you are sure you can contain them, put up with the lethal stems and prevent them from becoming a nuisance.

> **Trivia**
> *Brambles are an important food source for brimstone, green hairstreak and speckled wood butterflies.*

S

❧ PRUNING MADE SIMPLE ❧

Evergreen hedges

Now that nesting birds should have moved on, it's a good time to trim evergreen hedges if you want a formal look.

With the growing season drawing to an end, the straight lines made now will remain until next spring. Make sure your cutting tools are sharp before you start because after several months of use since spring, they may not be giving a clean cut, which could provide an entry point for disease.

❧ RECYCLING PROJECT ❧

Welly planters
Old wellies that are no longer wearable can live on as garden features – and if it's a hole in the sole that's finished them off then, hey presto, you've already got drainage. Wash them out, then get creative! Hang them from hooks in fence panels or on trellis if you've got a few that you want to show off as a fun feature. Use a drill to make more holes in the sole to let water escape easily.

❧ CROP OF THE MONTH ❧

Marrows
While harvesting courgette plants when the fruits are young and tender ensures a continuous crop, leaving some to become marrows this month gives a heavyweight harvest late in the growing season. This results in some impressive-looking fruits if you grow

Trivia
The record for the world's heaviest marrow is 116.4kg (256lb 10oz). It was grown by Vincent Sjodin and exhibited at the National Giant Vegetables Championship, Malvern, UK, in September 2021.

a stripey form such as 'Bush Baby'. In my experience, yellow courgettes tend to go hard in the centre if left to get large, so are best cropped when small.

HOUSEPLANT
∾ OF THE MONTH ∾

String of pearls
This slightly strange-looking trailing plant (*Senecio rowleyanus*) is perfect for growing on a shelf or in a hanging planter. It's a succulent, which tends to be good news for the less attentive houseplant curator. A watering every couple of weeks or so is a good rule of thumb. Wait for the compost to go dry and dusty before giving it a gentle watering, not allowing water to gather in the saucer below. Place in a bright spot out of direct sun and keep at a temperature of at least 13°C (55°F) in winter and ideally 21–24°C (70–75°F) in summer.

∾ HOW TO HELP WILDLIFE ∾

S

Leave a wild corner
Now is a good time to leave a corner of the garden wild to provide shelter for wildlife. If you have a grassy area, leave the grass unmown and start piling up logs or prunings from the garden. This could attract hedgehogs, while piles of fallen leaves, twigs and pine cones placed among piles of logs will make a nice bug hotel.

❧ BIRD OF THE MONTH ❧

Chiffchaff

This small warbler is very similar in appearance to the
willow warbler – they are around the same size and both
have olive-coloured bodies – but it's the song (as well as
its darker legs) that gives this bird away, with its squeaking
'chiff-chaff, chiff-chaff' from the treetops. Most chiffchaffs
are migrants from Africa, although some stay here all year
long, and they feed on flies, gnats and caterpillars, nesting
close to the ground in dense scrub.

WILD IN THE GARDEN
❧ THIS MONTH ❧

Common darter dragonfly

If you've got a pond in your garden then this is the dragonfly
that you are most likely to see. It gets its name from the way

that it darts forwards to catch insects. The males are bright red, and the females and immature adults are golden brown. As well as by water, look out for it perching on fence posts and plants, angling its wings towards the sun.

ANNUAL EVENTS AND
❧ HIGHLIGHTS ❧

National Organic Month
This is a celebration of organic food and drink, encouraging shoppers and gardeners to embrace products that are free from potentially harmful chemicals.

Heritage Open Days Festival
A packed programme of special events and activities takes place this month for England's largest festival of history and culture, with free entry for many of the National Trust's most famous attractions.

RHS Garden Wisley Flower Show, 2–7 September
An exciting mix of inspirational floral displays, specialist nurseries and expert advice to finish summer on a high note. There are also live talks from a range of experts at RHS Hilltop, The Home of Gardening Science at Wisley.

S

Harrogate Autumn Flower Show, 12–14 September
A rich celebration of gardening in autumn, with a wide range of seasonal flowers from specialist nurseries, as well as top-quality displays of exhibition vegetables and the ever-popular heaviest onion competition! Will the world record be broken in 2025?

Malvern Autumn Show, 26–28 September

Lots of autumn highlights are on show here, from giant vegetables to the RHS Floral Marquee packed with beautifully grown autumnal plants. Talks from expert gardeners and demonstrations in the cookery theatre make it a packed show, and don't miss the chance to take home some top-quality bulbs from specialist growers.

❧ GARDENER'S CHECKLIST ❧

☐ Net ponds to prevent leaf debris from entering the water.

☐ Harvest sweetcorn – it's ready if the kernels release a milky sap when squashed.

☐ Place pumpkin fruits on a paving slab or piece of wood to prevent skins from rotting.

☐ Pick blackberries, then prune off the fruited canes at ground level after harvest.

☐ Close greenhouse vents in the afternoon to lock in heat.

☐ Aerate well-trodden areas of lawn using a garden fork or hollow-tine aerator.

YOUR NOTES FOR
∽ SEPTEMBER ∾

To sow

To plant

In flower

Wildlife spotted

S

Beetroots

October

'With memories of summer fading fast and autumn well ensconced, it is sometimes easy to forget what a brilliant month October can be.'
– Carol Klein

O

A switch happens in October and it's well before the clocks go back. All of a sudden, attention turns towards preparation for the year to come, rather than preservation of what is happening in the present. Space needs to be found for spring bulbs; soil in the veg garden, exhausted from a year's cropping, is begging for a new layer of organic material; no sooner does it seem that this year's onions have been gathered, than it's time to plant another lot. At the start of the month, thoughts of starting things off for next year might seem a bit strange. But by the end, with summer's glory – and its harvests – fading fast, it makes perfect sense.

❧ SUNRISE AND SUNSET 2025 ❧

Location	Date	Rise	Set
Belfast			
	Oct 01 (Wed)	06:26 BST	17:59 BST
	Oct 11 (Sat)	06:45 BST	17:34 BST
	Oct 21 (Tue)	07:04 BST	17:11 BST
	Oct 31 (Fri)	07:24 GMT	16:49 GMT
Cardiff			
	Oct 01 (Wed)	06:13 BST	17:50 BST
	Oct 11 (Sat)	06:30 BST	17:27 BST
	Oct 21 (Tue)	06:47 BST	17:06 BST
	Oct 31 (Fri)	07:04 GMT	16:47 GMT
Edinburgh			
	Oct 01 (Wed)	06:16 BST	17:47 BST
	Oct 11 (Sat)	06:36 BST	17:21 BST
	Oct 21 (Tue)	06:56 BST	16:57 BST
	Oct 31 (Fri)	07:17 GMT	16:34 GMT
London			
	Oct 01 (Wed)	06:01 BST	17:37 BST
	Oct 11 (Sat)	06:18 BST	17:15 BST
	Oct 21 (Tue)	06:35 BST	16:54 BST
	Oct 31 (Fri)	06:52 GMT	16:34 GMT

O

❧ WEATHER CHARTS ❧

October averages 1991–2020

Location

Belfast	Max temperature (°C)	13.80
	Min temperature (°C)	6.92
	Days of air frost (days)	0.60
	Sunshine (hours)	92.36
	Rainfall (mm)	95.83
	Days of rainfall ≥1 mm (days)	13.77
Cardiff	Max temperature (°C)	15.25
	Min temperature (°C)	7.99
	Days of air frost (days)	0.93
	Sunshine (hours)	103.87
	Rainfall (mm)	129.05
	Days of rainfall ≥1 mm (days)	15.03
Edinburgh	Max temperature (°C)	13.37
	Min temperature (°C)	6.72
	Days of air frost (days)	1.27
	Sunshine (hours)	99.35
	Rainfall (mm)	75.71
	Days of rainfall ≥1 mm (days)	11.73
London	Max temperature (°C)	14.83
	Min temperature (°C)	8.34
	Days of air frost (days)	0.33
	Sunshine (hours)	106.29
	Rainfall (mm)	78.57
	Days of rainfall ≥1 mm (days)	11.03

❧ TASKS ❧

Things to start

Spring cabbages
It's a long wait for these succulent spring brassicas to mature, but they don't need much looking after. If you plant out good-sized ones, they will establish quickly this month and should be left alone by slugs once they have grown into substantial plants. Cover them with netting to keep pigeons at bay, and you can more or less forget about them apart from checking that they are well anchored, and perhaps firming them in some more with your foot if they look a bit wind beaten.

Overwintering peas
If your soil is very free-draining (and I mean so free-draining that you despair of it in summer and never see so much as a puddle after rainfall) then autumn-sown pea varieties such as 'Meteor' and 'Douce Provence' can be sown in a sheltered spot outside. But if you are unsure, start them off in lengths of guttering, in deep root trainers in a cold greenhouse, or on a windowsill indoors. These peas can be ready to harvest before May is out, giving you an extra batch of fresh pods to pick. Plant two seeds in each cell if growing in root trainers, or space them 2.5cm (1in) apart in the guttering.

O

> *'The softened light, the veiling haze,*
> *The calm repose of autumn days,*
> *Steal gently o'er the troubled breast,*
> *Soothing life's weary cares to rest.'*
>
> – From 'A Song for October' by Phoebe A. Holder

Things to finish

Quince

While apples and pears seem to like to tease us when it comes to ripeness, looking ready for weeks and weeks before being truly fit for picking, quinces announce that they are ready by releasing their intriguing aroma. Gently twist them from the tree, making sure you gather them before frost can spoil the fruits. Store in trays in a cool, unheated room, with the fruits not touching one another. Use strips of card as dividers. They can keep for 6–8 weeks this way.

Runner beans

There is a sadness about picking the last of the runner beans, but they do warn us a week or two before. Those long green pods that seem to appear from nowhere overnight are not in such abundant supply in September and there comes a point this month when you know it's over – usually when a cold night spoils a cluster of pods. It's a fond farewell to such a well-loved veg patch landmark, but I find it best to ditch the sentiment, pull up the canes, cut all the old growth from them and compost as soon as possible. The sight of shrivelled bean plants clinging to creaking supports at the end of autumn is a sad one that I'd rather replace with bare soil, topped up with a layer of compost to put some goodness back after a productive summer.

✧ SOMETHING TO SAVOUR ✧

Blazing blueberries

The autumn colour on blueberries is so good – good enough for them to be grown as ornamentals. This also serves as solace if it's been a poor year for the fruits, either because birds got there first or because your plants were young and still becoming established (blueberries with thin, twiggy growth will not be very productive). 'Collins' and 'Goldtraube' are good choices for autumn colour, and a quick hand-weed around the base of the plant followed by a mulch with ericaceous compost will make sure that the autumn display looks as good as possible.

Trivia
Blueberries make a good natural dye and early American settlers made grey paint by boiling blueberries in milk!

HEAD GARDENER'S PLANT
✧ OF THE MONTH – OCTOBER ✧ O

Salvia 'Phyllis Fancy' chosen by Catrina Saunders, Head Gardener at Trengwainton, Cornwall

Trengwainton's walled gardens are divided into ten sections, with the lower five entirely devoted to ornamental plants.

Salvia 'Phyllis Fancy' is in the centre section where it has both warmth and light. Salvias are generally late flowering, and this one is no exception, only really coming into full bloom in September. It has pale lavender blue flowers, with darker mauve calyces. These remain long after the flower has faded and give it an exceptionally long period of interest; we're still admiring it in the garden in December if the weather stays mild.

Give it as much sunshine and shelter as possible, and a well-drained, dry and gritty soil and it will thrive. These conditions will also give it the best opportunity for early flowering, which will then continue for the rest of the growing season.

This is a tender plant although if grown in the south west of the country it may come through the winter with the help of a rough mulch, and will then need cutting back in spring. No matter how scruffy it is over winter, don't be tempted to tidy it up too early as those old shoots are protective. We always take semi-ripe cuttings in August to ensure that we have a stock of these plants for the following year. If you leave collecting these until the autumn it becomes very hard to find any good shoots that will make cuttings material, because all the shoots are getting ready to flower.

IF YOU ONLY DO
∾ ONE THING... ∾

Make a layered bulb pot
A 'lasagne' pot (don't worry, there's no tomato sauce involved) is a great feature to make if you've not got room to

grow spring bulbs but don't want to miss out on the colour and excitement they bring as a new growing season begins.

- Half-fill a large pot with multi-purpose compost and place some tulip bulbs on the surface, close but not touching.
- Cover them with a 5cm (2in) layer of compost, then place your daffodil bulbs on the compost surface and cover them with another 5cm (2in) of compost.
- Plant the crocuses next and cover again with a slightly shallower compost layer.
- Cover the surface with a layer of grit and water well, then place in a sheltered, sunny corner.

❧ PRUNING MADE SIMPLE ❧

Asparagus

This is a nice and easy crop to sort out. Just cut each stem back to 3cm (1½in) from the base once the foliage has all turned yellow. Use sharp secateurs for cutting back and avoid pruning lightly because the old stems can harbour asparagus beetle; it also makes harvesting more difficult if long, woody stubs are left intact.

❧ RECYCLING PROJECT ❧

Plant up an old chair

If you've got an old dining chair that's destined for the tip because the upholstery has spoiled, perhaps it could be repurposed as a garden feature. Remove the cushioned part of the seat and you may simply be able to drop a large pot into the gap if it's wide enough. Or, if you can fit in a shallow tray instead, try filling this with gritty compost and planting it up with succulents. Before planting, consider sanding down the frame of the chair and giving it a couple of coats of coloured wood stain to add an extra pop of colour to the patio.

❧ CROP OF THE MONTH ❧

Beetroot

There are few crops that make life as easy for the gardener as beetroot. It isn't really troubled by pests; its clusters of seeds are very easy to sow; you can start new crops from March to July; and you can harvest them at any point when the roots are big enough for your liking. They turn mushy in winter once the weather gets wet and frosts arrive, so this month is a good time to gather what's left of your crop. If you've got a lot,

Trivia
An ancient Assyrian text, dating back to 800 BC describes beetroot plants in the Hanging Gardens of Babylon, one of the Seven Wonders of the Ancient World, and said to have been situated near present-day Hillah, central Iraq.

store them in trays of sand in a cool, dark place. Use up small roots rather than storing them because they will quickly shrivel in storage.

HOUSEPLANT
❧ OF THE MONTH ❧

Tradescantia albiflora 'Nanouk'
A gently tumbling evergreen with exciting foliage that looks great in a hanging planter, its stripy green, pink and white variegated leaves flushed with pinkish-purple underneath. Grow in bright light out of direct sun and water each time the compost has turned pale and dry. Push your finger into the compost, and if it's dry all the way down, then it needs some water. Very easy to propagate by snipping the ends of stems and pushing them into some compost.

❧ HOW TO HELP WILDLIFE ❧

Put up a nest box
It may seem like a strange time of year to put up a nest box, but doing it now will give resident garden birds the chance to use it as a roosting site for the winter to shelter from cold weather. You may get several birds staying in it on particularly cold nights. It also increases the chances of the box being used in spring. Make sure you put it up somewhere sheltered from the prevailing wind, around 3m (10ft) from ground level, and with a clear flight path around the entrance hole.

O

⤖ BIRD OF THE MONTH ⤕

Jay

This is a busy month for jays – screeching birds notable for their distinctive, beautiful azure-blue and black wing feathers – as they forage and bury acorns. Jays are quite shy, spending most of their time in hiding, but an absence of acorns to feed on and store for winter can see them venture into gardens to look for food.

Trivia
The Latin name for jays is Garrulus glandarius. *The word* garrulus *means 'noisy' and* glandarius *means 'of acorns'.*

WILD IN THE GARDEN ⤖ THIS MONTH ⤕

Orb weaver spider

These spiders are busy weaving their webs all through the garden, creators of what we probably consider to be a 'classic' spider's web. I often discover some fine patterns between the railings of my front garden gate, and if we get an early frost it's a real treat to see these works of art highlighted in all their glistening glory. The orb weavers sit inside the web until they hear the vibrations of another insect touching it. Then they wrap the intruder in silk and finish them off!

ANNUAL EVENTS AND
❧ HIGHLIGHTS ❧

Seed Gathering Season
Organised by the Tree Council, this is a time to remember to collect tree seeds and start growing the trees of the future – look out for events organised by your local Tree Warden Network.

RHS Harlow Carr Autumn Garden Weekend, 17–19 October
A range of exhibitors and nurseries visit the beautiful 23-ha (58-acre) garden in Harrogate for this special event, which includes talks, garden tours and live music.

Apple Day, 21 October
A celebration of the vast number of different apples grown in the UK. Pay a visit to some National Trust gardens with orchards, such as Cotehele in Cornwall with its historic Old

Orchard, or Coughton Court in Warwickshire – it's a great chance to broaden your horizons and get a taste for apples other than 'Braeburn' or 'Granny Smith'. Some varieties may even be local to your area.

'Playing with colour and form in the garden is the nearest that most of us will ever get to painting.'
– Mary Keen

❧ GARDENER'S CHECKLIST ❧

☐ Collect seed from perennials and annuals.

☐ Take hardwood cuttings of shrubs, roses and fruit bushes.

☐ Empty out summer containers that are past their best, ready for new displays for autumn and winter.

☐ Cover late-sown salads with cloches to keep them growing well.

☐ Lift and divide congested herbaceous perennials.

☐ Cover cauliflowers with fleece to protect the heads from frost damage.

YOUR NOTES FOR
∞ OCTOBER ∞

To sow

To plant

In flower

Wildlife spotted

O

Dog rose

November

'*I cannot endure wasting anything so precious as autumnal sunshine by staying in the house.*'
– Nathaniel Hawthorne

November is probably the month that arrives with the least excitement, despite the potential for trees showing off some fiery hues. The clocks have gone back, the heating's gone on, the garden is soggy, and there's no guarantee of frost to at least make your scruffy, ageing plants look pretty. Still, rather than bemoaning the state of the calendar, it's a good month to be a gardener because there are plenty of positive things to do to both cheer up the present and the future. It's the perfect month to plant tulips, and daffodil bulbs can still go in. Garlic and onions can be started off too. Perhaps in no other month does an instantly planted container bring more joy. It's amazing how a fern, a colourful sedge, a skimmia or a conifer, perhaps decorated with a trailing holly or periwinkle, can cheer the place up.

❧ SUNRISE AND SUNSET 2025 ❧

Location	Date	Rise	Set
Belfast			
	Nov 01 (Sat)	07:26 GMT	16:47 GMT
	Nov 11 (Tue)	07:46 GMT	16:28 GMT
	Nov 21 (Fri)	08:05 GMT	16:13 GMT
	Nov 30 (Sun)	08:21 GMT	16:03 GMT
Cardiff			
	Nov 01 (Sat)	07:06 GMT	16:45 GMT
	Nov 11 (Tue)	07:24 GMT	16:28 GMT
	Nov 21 (Fri)	07:41 GMT	16:15 GMT
	Nov 30 (Sun)	07:54 GMT	16:07 GMT
Edinburgh			
	Nov 01 (Sat)	07:20 GMT	16:31 GMT
	Nov 11 (Tue)	07:41 GMT	16:11 GMT
	Nov 21 (Fri)	08:01 GMT	15:55 GMT
	Nov 30 (Sun)	08:17 GMT	15:44 GMT
London			
	Nov 01 (Sat)	06:54 GMT	16:33 GMT
	Nov 11 (Tue)	07:11 GMT	16:16 GMT
	Nov 21 (Fri)	07:28 GMT	16:03 GMT
	Nov 30 (Sun)	07:42 GMT	15:55 GMT

N

❧ WEATHER CHARTS ❧

November averages 1991–2020

Location

Belfast	Max temperature (°C)	10.67
	Min temperature (°C)	4.18
	Days of air frost (days)	3.74
	Sunshine (hours)	52.87
	Rainfall (mm)	102.34
	Days of rainfall ≥1 mm (days)	15.52

Cardiff	Max temperature (°C)	11.61
	Min temperature (°C)	4.87
	Days of air frost (days)	3.66
	Sunshine (hours)	65.02
	Rainfall (mm)	130.65
	Days of rainfall ≥1 mm (days)	15.60

Edinburgh	Max temperature (°C)	9.86
	Min temperature (°C)	3.77
	Days of air frost (days)	5.27
	Sunshine (hours)	72.13
	Rainfall (mm)	65.25
	Days of rainfall ≥1 mm (days)	11.70

London	Max temperature (°C)	10.60
	Min temperature (°C)	5.04
	Days of air frost (days)	2.41
	Sunshine (hours)	67.19
	Rainfall (mm)	75.71
	Days of rainfall ≥1 mm (days)	11.93

❧ TASKS ❧

Things to start

Mushrooms

If you feel like having a go at growing mushrooms, the good news is that you can start a crop at any time of year. The easiest way to start is by buying a mushroom-growing kit from a reputable supplier. As is the case with many vegetables, growing your own at home gives you the chance to try types that are not easily available, or are very expensive in the shops. Shiitake, pink oyster, yellow oyster and lion's mane mushrooms can all be grown from kits. You could even hang them in a macramé planter and make them a feature. They take up little space, and when cropping is over, the spent compost can be added to your garden soil, and you may get some more mushrooms developing from the compost too. Before you start, make sure you've got a good misting bottle (some kits come with them), because the fungi will need regular misting to keep them hydrated and growing well.

> **Trivia**
> Mushrooms are a great source of vitamin D, absorbing the vitamin when exposed to sunlight or UV radiation.

Hedge planting

Starting a new hedge from bare-root 'whips' (young plants that look like bare twigs and are bought in soil-less, pot-less bundles) is a job that only takes minutes but can provide decades of joy. A mixed hedge of maple, hawthorn, blackthorn, guelder rose and dog rose will serve as a windbreak and multi-faceted wildlife station for years to

N

come. Whips (available from mail-order hedging companies) are planted by making a slit in the soil with a spade and wobbling it a bit to widen it. Drop the whips in and firm the soil well. The key to a hedge getting off to a good start is keeping it well watered and weed-free during the first spring and summer. Mulch with homemade compost after planting and you're well on your way. Few jobs in the garden will give such long-term satisfaction. Take some pictures of these unpromising-looking twigs, standing proud in defiance of a dull day in the month when autumn collides with winter. An unbelievable transformation is about to begin.

Things to finish

Winter squashes
Now's the last chance to bring in this super-heavy harvest before the frosts arrive and potentially damage the fruits. Put them in a conservatory or on a well-lit windowsill to allow the skins to harden for a couple of weeks after cutting them

from the plant, leaving around 10cm (4in) of stalk at the top of the fruit intact. Store them in an airy place at around 10°C (50°F) and they should keep until the end of winter. Keep giving the skins a pinch and if any start to feel soft, use these first.

Winter protection
Make sure all your plant protection measures are in place early this month. It's not just exotic feature plants such as bananas and tree ferns that benefit from a winter tuck-up. Perennials that are 'borderline hardy', such as *Salvia* 'Hot Lips' and 'Amistad', are best mulched with a 5–8cm (2–3in) layer of dry compost spread around the base of the plant, to prevent it from becoming too wet once the weather turns much colder. Pelargoniums and half-hardy fuchsias in pots can sometimes get through a mild winter if left outside, but it's safer to move them into a cold greenhouse and cover them with fleece on very cold nights. You can also keep them in a porch or on a well-lit kitchen windowsill.

❧ SOMETHING TO SAVOUR ❧

Trees
It's easier than ever to notice trees in autumn, as so many leaves start to put on a multi-coloured show as the low sun catches them. Even something as seemingly functional as a beech hedge can become a glowing thing of wonder. It's well worth the effort to visit National Trust gardens or parkland to see some spectacular trees in their autumn finery and get a big autumn colour fix.

N

HEAD GARDENER'S PLANT
∾ OF THE MONTH – NOVEMBER ∾

Fuchsia microphylla **chosen by Paul Walton, Head Gardener at Biddulph Grange, Staffordshire**

We grow these delightfully adaptable plants in huge terracotta pots on our Italian Terrace. The delicate flowers complement the spring bulbs and summer bedding that we plant in this area every year. They are also planted in the borders surrounding our Verbena Parterre, where we grow a range of different fuchsia species.

The flowering period is so long that this could be a plant of the month during most months of the year! The tiny, bright magenta flowers are hard to resist; they look so fragile, yet it's one of the few plants which will flower right up until we have a hard frost.

Fuchsia microphylla is such an easy-going plant – it has no preference regarding pH or soil type, as long as the soil is moist and well-drained. Like all fuchsias, it likes to be in the sun, but because of its small leaves, it needs to be given a bit of shelter from any drying winds.

It's such a reliable performer with no special requirements or treatment. The pots on the terrace are included in our regular watering and feeding routine for all containers during the summer and autumn. As a late-flowering shrub, it can be left over winter and then given a prune in early spring to encourage growth.

IF YOU ONLY DO
↝ ONE THING... ↜

Order bare-root plants

Bare-root plants are ideal if you need to add a quantity of roses, hedging or fruit trees to the garden, because large numbers can be transported into a small space, tied up in twiggy bundles, with no pots or compost needed. It is also a good way of buying if you are looking for unusual varieties because there is often a wider selection if you buy bare-root. With this in mind, now is a good time to order, before rare varieties sell out. The other advantage of buying plants this way is that you are getting the 'pick of the crop': young, vigorous plants freshly lifted from fields where they have been able to develop without the restrictions of a pot.

↝ PRUNING MADE SIMPLE ↜

Blueberries

Blueberries are one of the less demanding garden fruits, as long as you remember to net the plants to protect the berries from birds. They don't need any complicated pruning to fruit well, but they can be given a tidy up now. Start by trimming out any very thin

Trivia
The blueberry variety 'Ozblu' is known for the exceptional size of its fruits. An Ozblu fruit weighing 16.2g (over ½oz), grown by David and Leasa Mazzardis in Wilbinga, Australia, is on record as the world's heaviest blueberry.

stems in the centre of the plant because they are unlikely
to mature into fruiting wood. Also, shorten any long, thick
stems by around one-third to encourage the plant to become
bushier. Trim any shoots that have died back, cutting into
green growth, and prune the ends of branches that fruited in
summer, taking them back to just above a strong bud. This
will encourage more fruiting sideshoots.

❧ RECYCLING PROJECT ❧

Make a compost bin out of pallets
Three old pallets, secured to the ground by knocking thick
stakes into each corner will make a useful enclosure for
your homemade compost, and provide a nice wide entrance
for both adding to it and shovelling the end product into a
wheelbarrow. You may need to dig over the ground first so
it's easier to knock in the stakes. You can secure the upright
pallets tightly by screwing them together where they join
using metal brackets. If you don't want to leave the front
open, add a fourth pallet and secure to one of the side pallets
by screwing on hinges, to make a front gate.

❧ CROP OF THE MONTH ❧

Carrots
If your soil drains well and your garden is in a mild area, you
can probably get away with leaving carrots in the ground
and lifting them up as and when you want them, especially
if you cover the tops with a layer of straw or fleece. If you've
managed to leave carrots in the ground this long, you should
have some pretty heavy roots to harvest. If they have been

a disappointment and produced misshapen roots that are good for little except a funniest vegetable competition, consider growing them in pots next year. Carrots will grow on heavy, stony soils, but they may struggle to develop properly, and can also be difficult to clean if they are full of nooks and crannies. Grown in pots of multi-purpose compost, you'll get clean, long, thick roots that are easy to prepare, provided you keep watering them in dry spells.

Trivia
Each year 22 billion carrot seeds are sown in Britain, resulting in a harvest equal to 100 carrots for every member of the population.

HOUSEPLANT
⮞ OF THE MONTH ⮜

Prayer plant
This increasingly popular, low-growing, variegated houseplant (*Maranta leuconeura*) is so-called because of the way that it closes up its leaves at night, like praying hands, before opening them up again when a new day begins. In the wild these plants smother the rainforest floor. They will develop spreading stems that are well shown off if placed in a pot on a shelf with plenty of space beneath it.

For growing success:
• Keep the compost moist at all times, not letting it dry out completely between watering but also not letting the roots stand in water.

N

- Keep in a warm room (ideally 16–24°C/61–75°F) and mist the plant daily if possible.
- Position the plant in a well-lit place but out of direct sunlight.

❧ HOW TO HELP WILDLIFE ❧

Make throughways for hedgehogs

Hedgehogs have some stamina, walking around 1 mile (1.6km) every night looking for food and a mate. If possible, help them along by providing safe passage between your garden and next door's. This can be done by cutting a square 13 × 13cm (5 × 5in) in the bottom of a fence panel in a sheltered corner of the garden. There are also hedgehog-friendly fence panels and gravel boards available with ready-formed holes.

❧ BIRD OF THE MONTH ❧

Waxwing

When food levels in Scandinavia and western Russia run low, this striking bird, with a magnificent crest that looks like it's taken a fair few hours to perfect in the salon, begins to head to the UK, particularly the eastern side. There may be thousands making the trip, or hardly any at all, depending on the availability of berries where they are. Its colouring is striking, a pinkish-buff body, with yellow-tipped tail feathers and tiny flashes of yellow and red on its wing. They are very partial to berries, especially those of the rowan tree (*Sorbus aucuparia*).

WILD IN THE GARDEN
❧ THIS MONTH ❧

Dog rose

This is a great choice for growing the bare-root way, with
bundles of plants sold for hedging at a reasonable price. Dog
roses (*Rosa canina*) offer a lot to a hedgerow, with elegant hot
pink blossom in summer, easily foraged by bees, followed
by cherry-red hips, which will be eyed-up by blackbirds as
well as squirrels and voles. The hips are very nutritious, rich
in vitamin C and can be used to make rosehip syrup to help
keep winter colds at bay.

ANNUAL EVENTS AND
❧ HIGHLIGHTS ❧

Guy Fawkes Night, 5 November

Coughton Court, Warwickshire, is the ideal place to learn
more about the notorious Gunpowder Plot. The ringleader
of the plot was Robert Catesby, son of Sir William Catesby
and Anne Throckmorton of Coughton Court. Find out
more by paying a visit and let a National Trust volunteer tell
you the story (check opening times before you travel).

Remembrance Sunday, 9 November

The world-famous Sandham Memorial Chapel in
Hampshire is open, along with the Garden of Reflection
planted by the National Trust in 2014 to mark the
centenary of the commencement of the First World War.

N

National Tree Week, 26 November–4 December
A nationwide event to celebrate the beginning of the tree-planting season and to acknowledge the role trees and woodland play in our lives. There will be events throughout the country to include talks, tree dressing and, of course, tree planting. Check your local National Trust property or estate to find out what's going on.

❧ GARDENER'S CHECKLIST ❦

☐ Start collecting wet fallen leaves to make leaf mould soil improver.

☐ Plant tulips in containers in sunny, sheltered parts of the garden.

☐ Cut back tall rose bushes to prevent them from wind damage.

☐ Cover brassicas with netting to protect them from pigeons.

☐ Lift and store dahlias and cannas once frost has spoilt the foliage.

☐ Bring potted herbs such as parsley and coriander indoors for winter.

YOUR NOTES FOR
❧ NOVEMBER ❧

To sow

To plant

In flower

Wildlife spotted

N

Holly

December

D

This is the month when it's easy to forget gardening altogether, but foraging for some festive greenery will help remind you that the garden is still there. As will a few frosty mornings when it's well worth getting out and seeing some of summer's most treasured plants transformed into ethereal artworks. There's also a chance this month that you may end up with more houseplants than you had before, whether you wanted them or not! Better to be the Scrooge at the end of *A Christmas Carol* rather than the one at its beginning and embrace them with gusto. A few amaryllis bulbs in particular will sharpen those gardening instincts and brighten up the house in a few weeks' time.

❧ SUNRISE AND SUNSET 2025 ❧

Location	Date	Rise	Set
Belfast			
	Dec 01 (Mon)	08:22 GMT	16:02 GMT
	Dec 11 (Thu)	08:36 GMT	15:57 GMT
	Dec 21 (Sun)	08:44 GMT	15:59 GMT
	Dec 31 (Wed)	08:46 GMT	16:07 GMT
Cardiff			
	Dec 01 (Mon)	07:56 GMT	16:07 GMT
	Dec 11 (Thu)	08:08 GMT	16:03 GMT
	Dec 21 (Sun)	08:15 GMT	16:05 GMT
	Dec 31 (Wed)	08:18 GMT	16:13 GMT
Edinburgh			
	Dec 01 (Mon)	08:19 GMT	15:43 GMT
	Dec 11 (Thu)	08:33 GMT	15:38 GMT
	Dec 21 (Sun)	08:42 GMT	15:39 GMT
	Dec 31 (Wed)	08:43 GMT	15:48 GMT
London			
	Dec 01 (Mon)	07:44 GMT	15:54 GMT
	Dec 11 (Thu)	07:56 GMT	15:51 GMT
	Dec 21 (Sun)	08:03 GMT	15:53 GMT
	Dec 31 (Wed)	08:06 GMT	16:01 GMT

D

❧ WEATHER CHARTS ❧

December averages 1991–2020

Location

Belfast	Max temperature (°C)	8.44
	Min temperature (°C)	2.26
	Days of air frost (days)	7.07
	Sunshine (hours)	35.31
	Rainfall (mm)	93.25
	Days of rainfall ≥1 mm (days)	14.83
Cardiff	Max temperature (°C)	9.06
	Min temperature (°C)	2.84
	Days of air frost (days)	7.95
	Sunshine (hours)	50.44
	Rainfall (mm)	139.58
	Days of rainfall ≥1 mm (days)	15.17
Edinburgh	Max temperature (°C)	7.34
	Min temperature (°C)	1.57
	Days of air frost (days)	10.4
	Sunshine (hours)	49.15
	Rainfall (mm)	67.43
	Days of rainfall ≥1 mm (days)	12.30
London	Max temperature (°C)	7.81
	Min temperature (°C)	2.71
	Days of air frost (days)	7.74
	Sunshine (hours)	54.01
	Rainfall (mm)	68.25
	Days of rainfall ≥1 mm (days)	11.86

❧ TASKS ❧

Things to start

Fruit trees

The thought of picking a plum or apple fresh from the tree
as summer turns to autumn probably feels light years away
this month, but if it's not frozen or too wet underfoot, it's
a great time to plant a fruit tree. Bare-root or potted ones
can be planted now so that they can get their roots well
established by the time spring arrives, with no damaging
heat to stress them.

- Make a hole the same depth as the roots and three times as
  wide; any deeper and the tree can 'sink' after planting.
- Place the tree in the hole and check the level so that the
  point where the base of the trunk meets the roots is level
  with the surface of the soil.
- Hold the tree upright and fill the hole with the soil that
  you dug out.
- Knock a stake into the ground at an angle in the direction
  of the prevailing wind and tie the tree to it using a rubber
  tie.
- Water the tree well until puddles form at the base of the
  plant, then spread a compost mulch 5cm (2in) thick on the
  soil, but not touching the tree.

Cut-and-come-again leaves

It may seem like a crazy thing to do but if you fill a 20cm
(8in) pot with multi-purpose compost that has been kept
indoors, sprinkle a salad leaf seed mix on the surface, and
cover with vermiculite or sieved compost, then a new salad
crop is underway. Keep the pot on a well-lit windowsill in

D

a room where the temperature is 16–21°C (61–70°F) and the crop will steadily grow in the coming weeks, giving you something to nurture during the cold months.

Things to finish

Leaf gathering

This month is the last chance to gather as many leaves as possible to create the garden gold-dust known as leaf mould. There is definitely strength in numbers with leaf gathering. The more fallen leaves you can collect in bins, heaps or even just bin bags, the more of this wonderful dark, crumbly soil improver you will have in a year or so. There's none of the delicate ingredient balancing that's required for making compost, and the breakdown of the leaves is more consistent than the components of compost, which all break down at their own pace and won't be rushed. The result is a finer, more regular substance that makes a wonderful base for homemade potting compost, mixed with equal parts homemade compost, or a terrific mulch for suppressing weeds and improving soil drainage.

Brussels sprouts

Bringing a bowlful of sprouts into the kitchen with fingers like blocks of ice after snapping them from their stalks is a feeling that goes back to my childhood on a farm. Braving the cold to capture this much-maligned veg might not fill you with excitement, but once they've been exposed to frost Brussels sprouts are one of the sweetest winter vegetables. Leave them intact on the stalks to pick as and when you want them so that you're cooking them at the peak of their freshness. Indoors they soon shrivel and turn yellow, but kept intact in the garden they will retain their firmness and vibrant green for much longer. The cabbage-like growth at the top of each plant is a tasty vegetable in its own right. Cut them off the top of the plant from October onwards and cook them like cabbage. Cover your sprouts with netting if it's very cold, as pigeons will be on the look-out for the last plants standing!

Trivia
The area of the UK dedicated to Brussels sprout fields is equal in size to 3,240 football pitches.

❧ SOMETHING TO SAVOUR ❧

Excellent evergreens

This is the month when the evergreens in your garden start to become more obvious than they have been since about April, when perennial plants were just slowly rising from ground level, and annuals were still seedlings in pots or even figments of your imagination. Enjoy them as living statues and use this month as a time to work out where you could plant more to add extra 'backbone' to the garden. *Sarcococca* 'Winter Gem' (a form of winter box) has sweetly scented flowers as well as dense evergreen foliage and would make a good choice for adding structure and fragrance by a path. It grows around 50cm (20in) tall and wide. Leave enough room so that it doesn't narrow the path or you'll be forever trimming it to make space.

D

HEAD GARDENER'S PLANT
❧ OF THE MONTH – DECEMBER ❧

Jasminum nudiflorum chosen by Ed Atkinson, Head
Gardener at Blickling Hall, Norfolk

If we are lucky with the weather towards the end of
December then one of my favourite plants is winter jasmine
(*Jasminum nudiflorum*). Its beautiful, small, yellow flowers,
although unscented like other jasmine varieties, really shine
against an otherwise drab background. In its native China it
is often called *yingchun*, the 'flower that welcomes spring'. It
can certainly lift the spirits post-Christmas.

At Blickling it grows along a north-facing wall in the West
Garden, sheltered by a large yew hedge, on the main route
from the Walled Garden to the Front Drive.

This variety will flower from late December right through
till March. *Nudiflorum*, which means 'naked flower', loves
to climb and will bring colour and impact over the winter
months. It's the hardiest of all jasmines and rarely lets you
down at this challenging time of year. It loves to be grown
against a sheltered wall that receives plenty of sunlight.

This jasmine responds well to regular pruning; prevent bare
patches by tying in the stems as it won't twine like other
varieties of jasmine. Alternatively, you can let it sprawl over a
low-lying wall or structure – it's a very forgiving plant so let
your imagination ramble, as it were.

> *'The twelve months ...*
> *Snowy, Flowy, Blowy,*
> *Showery, Flowery, Bowery,*
> *Hoppy, Croppy, Droppy,*
> *Breezy, Sneezy, Freezy.'*
> – George Ellis

IF YOU ONLY DO
❧ ONE THING... ❦

Plant a mixed winter pot

There comes a point in early December when I decide enough is enough and to lift the gloom of all those wet and dull days, I plant up some new pots. I never tire of giving the patio an instant lift, and I like to use only plants that can have another life planted out in the garden later, or that can stay in the pot for more than one year. There are lots of familiar plants being pushed in the garden centres, from skimmias to ivies and conifers, but get creative and don't be afraid to go off piste! Try matching some colourful-leaved heucheras with winter-flowering violas. Or try a brilliant evergreen grass such as *Carex testacea* or *Carex oshimensis* 'Everillo'. Push a few tulip bulbs into any gaps in the compost to inject an extra burst of colour to welcome the spring.

D

❧ PRUNING MADE SIMPLE ❧

Apple trees

Established apple trees grown as traditional upright trees (rather than being trained against walls or wires) are best pruned in winter to keep them productive, so the majority of the growth on the tree is young and fruitful. Make sure your cutting tools are sharp and clean before you start.

- Aim to prune to open up the framework of branches in the centre of the tree by removing any that are crossing into others or rubbing against a neighbouring branch. This will allow more sunlight to reach developing fruits.
- Remove stems showing signs of disease, cutting back into clean wood.
- Shorten long growths made this year to encourage fruiting spurs to develop.
- Avoid over-pruning the tree because it will result in a mass of new twiggy growth next year.

❧ RECYCLING PROJECT ❧

Use old corks to mulch pots

To add an extra detail to feature plants in pots on the patio or a houseplant or two, try using wine corks as a mulch. If there is enough space between the rim of the pot and the compost surface, place them upright and pack them in to make a solid surface. Water will still be able to reach the plant, and because corks don't hold on to water, they won't decompose either. If the corks are too tall and above the pot rim, you can cut them to size. Put them into boiling water for ten minutes, take them out and they will be easy to cut.

HOUSEPLANT
❧ OF THE MONTH ❧

Christmas cactus

This attractive evergreen (*Schlumbergera truncata*) is a much more reliable and easy-to-grow festive houseplant than a poinsettia, and for a similar price it can brighten up your home for years with exotic flowers in hot pink, red, yellow, or even white. It's also easy to propagate from cuttings taken in spring. Use a cutting with three leaf sections on it, let it dry indoors for a couple of days, then insert it to a depth of 1cm (½in) into pots of gritty compost and keep on a bright windowsill away from full sun. This is the best place to keep a mature plant too, at 18–24°C (75°F). Move the plant somewhere cooler (at around 12°C/54°F) for a couple

D

of months after flowering, and water sparingly, before putting it back in its normal place. Then do it all again in September, before moving it back as flower buds start to form on the end of the stems. Feed with a general houseplant food once a month from spring until the end of summer.

Trivia
In the wild, Christmas cactus grows in rainforests in Brazil. It roots itself on debris that has gathered in living trees or grows in crevices in rocks, meaning that its home environment is very different from desert-dwelling cacti.

❧ CROP OF THE MONTH ❧

Winter lettuce

Having a crisp lettuce to pick at this time of year is a real treat, and perhaps one of those achievements it's hard not to feel a little smug about, simply because it feels so 'out of season' to be doing it. Before picking, give each lettuce a little squeeze and if it feels firm, twist it to remove it from the soil. Leave the others to grow on, and if growing in a greenhouse border, keep watering with tepid water if the soil dries out. Keep winter lettuces outside covered with cloches until you are ready to harvest them.

❧ HOW TO HELP WILDLIFE ❧

Put out water for birds

Providing clean water will help the bird population that visits your garden to stay healthy. A source of fresh water is a lifeline for garden birds, especially in freezing conditions when they would have to use significant energy trying to access water. If bird baths are frozen, break the ice or thaw it with hot (but not boiling) water from a kettle, then add some fresh, clean water. Place the bird bath in a position where it will receive direct sun to reduce the length of time that the water is frozen, and keep the bath full, which will make it slower to freeze over. To be of maximum use, a bird bath needs to have shallow, sloping sides and a water depth of 2.5–10cm (1–4in).

D

❧ BIRD OF THE MONTH ❧

Robin

Surely the most recognisable garden bird, perhaps not just for the distinctive red breast of the adult males and females, but for their seemingly constant activity and boldness. They are in song for most of the year and I hear their optimistic tweeting from my office window on many a dark winter's night, wondering 'Why are you up so late?' As well as resident birds being regulars on bird tables this month, they are likely to be joined by migratory robins from northern and eastern Europe too.

Trivia

Robins can begin building nests as early as January if the weather is mild, although the breeding season usually begins in March.

WILD IN THE GARDEN ❧ THIS MONTH ❧

Winter gnats

On a still day you may see a swarm of these insects, similar in appearance to craneflies, but smaller. Males gather together and dance in the winter sun to attract the females, and are most likely to be seen in damp parts of the garden that are rich in humus – so you may well encounter them around your compost heap.

ANNUAL EVENTS AND
❧ HIGHLIGHTS ❧

Tree Dressing Day, 6–7 December
A practice celebrated all over the world, tree dressing helps highlight the important role that trees play in our lives. Look out for opportunities to get involved in your local community, with schools encouraged to take part.

Christmas events
Many National Trust properties are a sight to behold this month, bedecked in their festive finery, and there are many special events taking place too. Soak up the sights, sounds, smells and flavours of the season at the Garden of

D

Lights event held at Blickling Hall, Norfolk, or experience
A Winter's Night inside Gunby Hall, Lincolnshire, with
creatively themed and decorated rooms.

Festival of Winter Walks
The Ramblers festival has been running (or should that be
walking) for more than 25 years. Look out for a group walk
near you or go on your own walk, exploring the library of
Ramblers Routes.

❧ GARDENER'S CHECKLIST ❧

☐ Take root cuttings of oriental poppies, verbascums
and echinops.

☐ Mulch 'borderline hardy' shrubs with a 5cm (2in)
layer of dry bark.

☐ Plant bare-root roses when it is dry enough
underfoot.

☐ Clear ground and cover soil ready for early spring
sowing.

☐ Cover celery with fleece and weigh it down with
bricks or bits of broken paving.

☐ Prune dead, damaged, diseased and crossing
growth from apple and pear trees.

YOUR NOTES FOR
❧ DECEMBER ❧

To sow

_____

_____

_____

_____

_____

To plant

_____

_____

_____

_____

_____

In flower

_____

_____

_____

_____

_____

Wildlife spotted

_____

_____

_____

_____

D

Index

219

223